ASHE Higher Education Report: Volume 38, Number 6
Kelly Ward, Lisa E. Wolf-Wendel, Series Editors

Immigrant Students and Higher Education

Eunyoung Kim

Jeannette Díaz

Discover this journal online at
WILEY ONLINE LIBRARY
wileyonlinelibrary.com

ɫ 8198 16 740

Immigrant Students and Higher Education
Eunyoung Kim and Jeannette Díaz
ASHE Higher Education Report: Volume 38, Number 6
Kelly Ward, Lisa E. Wolf-Wendel, Series Editors

Cover image by a_Taiga/©iStockphoto.

ISSN 1551-6970   electronic ISSN 1554-6306   ISBN 978-1-1186-1415-0

The ASHE Higher Education Report is part of the Jossey-Bass Higher and Adult Education Series and is published six times a year by Wiley Subscription Services, Inc., A Wiley Company, at Jossey-Bass, One Montgomery Street, Suite 1200, San Francisco, California 94104-4594.

Individual subscription rate (in USD): $174 per year US/Can/Mex, $210 rest of world; institutional subscription rate: $307 US, $367 Can/Mex, $418 rest of world. Single copy rate: $29. Electronic only–all regions: $174 individual, $307 institutional; Print & Electronic–US: $192 individual, $353 institutional; Print & Electronic–Canada/Mexico: $192 individual, $413 institutional; Print & Electronic–Rest of World: $228 individual, $464 institutional. See the Back Issue/Subscription Order Form in the back of this volume.

CALL FOR PROPOSALS: Prospective authors are strongly encouraged to contact Kelly Ward (kaward@wsu.edu) or Lisa Wolf-Wendel (lwolf@ku.edu). See "About the ASHE Higher Education Report Series" in the back of this volume.

Visit the Jossey-Bass Web site at **www.josseybass.com.**

Printed in the United States of America on acid-free recycled paper.

The ASHE Higher Education Report is indexed in CIJE: Current Index to Journals in Education (ERIC), Education Index/Abstracts (H.W. Wilson), ERIC Database (Education Resources Information Center), Higher Education Abstracts (Claremont Graduate University), IBR & IBZ: International Bibliographies of Periodical Literature (K.G. Saur), and Resources in Education (ERIC).

Advisory Board

The ASHE Higher Education Report Series is sponsored by the Association for the Study of Higher Education (ASHE), which provides an editorial advisory board of ASHE members.

Contents

Executive Summary

Immigrants have profoundly transformed the demographic landscape and economic structure of America. Reaching almost 40 million and accounting for nearly 13 percent of the entire U.S. population in 2010 (Camarota, 2011; Passel and Cohn, 2012), the immigrant population continues to grow. More than one out of five students enrolled in U.S. postsecondary institutions are immigrants, but there is a scarcity of research informing a comprehensive understanding of the educational experiences and outcomes of these students. The immigrant student population in higher education is underexamined, inaccurately characterized, and often misunderstood. Thus, the purpose of this monograph is to synthesize the current body of research on immigrant students and lay a foundation for future research on the growing presence of these students in higher education. For the purposes of this monograph, the term *immigrant student* or *immigrant-origin student* broadly refers to students who have moved to the United States from abroad at some point in their lives and (intend to) live here permanently *as well as* those who were born in the United States with at least one foreign-born parent. Bearing in mind that there is no uniform definition of immigrant employed by policymakers and educational researchers, we propose a conceptual model that captures three core dimensions along which to define the term *immigrant:* (1) nativity, (2) immigrant status, and (3) generational status.

Educational Attainment and Occupational Outcomes of Immigrants

Overall, the foreign-born population's educational attainment and labor market participation are relatively lower than those of the native-born. More important, educational attainment and employment vary to a considerable extent by race/ethnicity, generational status, immigrant status, and country of origin. Thus, it is important to make it clear that the educational and occupational outcomes for immigrants can be understood only by looking at a complex socioeconomic landscape that includes not only demographic considerations but also the population's fundamental heterogeneity.

Conceptual Frameworks for Understanding the Educational Experiences of Immigrant Students

Building theoretical underpinnings that adequately explore the multiplicity of immigrant students' experiences and contexts is necessary to the development and implementation of effective policy, practice, and research in higher education. This monograph introduces and discusses four conceptual frameworks useful for examining the educational experiences of immigrant-origin students and the varied dimensions of life that shape their college transitions and collegiate experiences: (1) neo-racism, (2) social-ecological perspectives, (3) acculturation and assimilation theories, and (4) social capital theory.

College Access and Success for Immigrant Students

After reviewing current literature, we identify multiple factors important to facilitating access to college among immigrant students including race/ethnicity, generational status, socioeconomic status, (limited) English language proficiency, parental expectations and involvement, and financial aid. However, scant research exists on which immigrant student groups actually transition to college, what educational experiences they have after matriculation, the challenges they face while in college, and to what extent postsecondary education outcomes differ across various immigrant student groups. Drawing on currently available literature on the educational experiences of immigrant college students, we organize our synthesis into four broad research themes: (1) college adjustment and persistence, (2) psychological development and acculturation, (3) social identity development, and (4) career aspirations and development. We also focus specifically on a distinctively disadvantaged immigrant student subpopulation, undocumented students, and some of the unique challenges faced by them.

Though research has demonstrated immigrant students' high motivation and positive trajectory of academic achievement, transition to postsecondary education, and degree attainment, there is a substantive gap in our understanding of the nuances of race, ethnicity, immigrant status, gender, age at immigration, as well as context variables such as immigration trends, institutional and public policy, and how these affect the experiences of immigrant college students.

The Future of Immigrants in Higher Education Research and Practice

Because higher education serves as a pathway for immigrants to integrate into American society, it has figured prominently in immigration reform debates. With many countries of origin, a wide geographic dispersion, and varying statuses of immigration, the diversity of the immigrant population, coupled with national and state immigration policies constantly in flux, poses a set of complex challenges to which higher education must respond (Fix and Passel, 2003). In particular, community colleges have been at the forefront in providing gateways to postsecondary education for diverse immigrant populations. However, there remains a lot more to learn about how multiple layers of context (for example, financial aid policy at the federal, state, and institutional level for undocumented immigrants) affect access to postsecondary education and educational outcomes for immigrants across different situations of race/ethnicity, immigrant status, generational status, country of origin, and social class. We acknowledge that one program, one definition, and one policy do not fit all. In order to better understand immigrant students' educational experiences, improve their educational opportunities, and help them become productive and engaged democratic citizens, we need to focus on how public and institutional policy toward admissions and financial aid affect immigrant students. We also need to look at how student affairs policy and practice, and institutional academic policies and curricula, influence immigrant students' development and growth. The increasingly diverse and multicultural visage of the college community, plus the growing number of immigrants on college campuses, raises questions about how—and how well—institutions help immigrants adapt to the college environment. To meet the educational needs of immigrant students, the higher education community must make a concerted effort to be more sensitive to immigration policy issues and cultural nuances among immigrant students and be more creative in their programmatic and intervention efforts to serve the unique set of challenges these students face.

Foreword

The terrain of international, immigrant, and undocumented students is of increasing importance given the globalized focused of American higher education and demographic realities of the population of the United States. As the face of American higher education and society changes, it is crucial to examine the educational experience for immigrants and students with a family of immigrant origins. A major challenge with meeting the needs of these students and with conducting sound research is the lack of a basic understanding of who these students are and how they are defined and served in research and practice.

Who are immigrant students? How do they differ from undocumented students? Are they international students? How do their different identities overlap? How are these students acknowledged in research? How are they served in practice? These and other questions provide a focal point for Eunyoung Kim and Jeannette Díaz's monograph, *Immigrant Students and Higher Education*. The authors make a key contribution to dialogue about students from immigrant and/or undocumented backgrounds first and foremost by providing definitions of the many categories and associated labels with students who fall into the very broad category of "immigrant" students.

Any student who is not a native-born U.S. citizen who enrolls in a college or university in the United States can be classified (rightly or wrongly) into categories like international, immigrant, and/or undocumented as a way to make sense of financial aid and other support services. The challenge in practice has been how to foster the success of students independent of their "category." In the research literature, the task is to unpack the different categories and student experiences and how they shape identity, which in many cases is overlapping and culturally defined. Naïve practice and research related to the broad category of immigrant students is problematic for the students themselves, the student service practitioners who work with them, the faculty who teach them, and the researchers who attempt to study and make meaning of their student experiences.

In this monograph, Kim and Díaz do a laudable job of first defining and teasing out the different categories related to immigrant students and what implications these definitions have for higher education. For administrators, faculty, and staff to fully recognize students from different backgrounds necessitates first understanding who the students are and their unique vantage point entering into higher education. It's not possible to homogenize the "immigrant" student experience given broad experiences related to family and educational background as well as socioeconomic status. It's not possible to disentangle these different aspects of student identity. An immigrant student who is enrolled in higher education who moved to the United States with his or her parents, who have assumed a high-level professional position and have work visas, is not the same as a student who moved to the United States with his or her parents who entered the country illegally. The circumstances of immigration very much dictate the experience students and their families are likely to have with higher education and must be acknowledged as part of the overall conversation related to immigrant students in higher education. John Ogbu (1990), in the journal article entitled "Minority Education in Comparative Perspectives" published in the *Journal of Negro Education*, was one of the first researchers to point out the importance of student background and how it shapes the student experience. Family background and culture are particularly relevant for students with immigration in their history. Ogbu's work highlights the importance of differences in family history related to immigration and also the reasons and financial circumstances of immigration. Forced immigration for financial or political reasons can sometimes lead to being in the United States under duress and sometimes mean parents are not financially secure. Clearly, these students would likely have a different experience than that of a student of an immigrant family background that is the consequence of job opportunities, which is different yet again from a student with an international background that involves multiple moves of migration. Yet research and practice has tended to cluster these students similarly as "immigrant students," perpetuating the homogenization of assumed experience of a very diverse group of students.

The monograph directly grapples with the definitional terrain as a way to highlight the need for new conceptual models to study immigrant students and the need for revised practices to improve student experiences. It is imperative for higher education researchers looking at the student experience for those from non–U.S. backgrounds and also for faculty and staff who work with these same students to fully understand the nuances of students with immigrant backgrounds. The issues are particularly germane given the legal terrain surrounding students and the support they receive based on their status with immigrant backgrounds. The monograph goes far beyond definition by providing theoretical perspectives and ideas for practice. The monograph also grapples with institutional type, especially the community college, which is often a pathway for immigrant students.

The monograph is related to several others in the series, including *Cultural and Social Capital* by Rachelle Winkle Wagner, as well as Marybeth Walpole's monograph, *Economically and Educationally Challenged Students in Higher Education*. Kim and Díaz's monograph on immigrant students is also a companion to forthcoming monographs on Latino/a students and Asian American students. Given that the identities of immigrant students overlap into cultural and socioeconomic status, it's helpful to look at these students mindful of the different backgrounds that shape research perspectives and the student experience. Student affairs practitioners, faculty, administrators, and researchers interested in different aspects of the student experience are sure to find this monograph useful to broaden perspectives in theory and practice.

Kelly Ward
Series Editor

Acknowledgments

This monograph would not have been conceivable without Martin Finkel-stien's guidance and support. Marty, thank you for being a great mentor, an insightful critic, and a kind colleague! You suffered graciously through some dreadful drafts early on, challenging me to think critically and work toward clarity and solidity. I'd like to thank Lisa Wolf-Wendel and Kelly Ward, who were committed to working with me throughout this monograph project. Thank you so much, Jeannette; you made important contributions to this monograph, particularly for the chapter "Undocumented Students and Higher Education." My colleagues at Seton Hall, especially the late Joseph DePierro (former dean) and my colleagues in the Department of Education Leadership, Management and Policy—you all have my appreciation as well. Many thanks go to my graduate assistant, Tharinee Kamnoetsin, who tire-lessly assisted me in the search for relevant literature and construction of a comprehensive bibliography. I'd also like to thank many graduate students in the college student personnel administration and higher education program, including Ann Szipszky. I am grateful to Natalie Mesnard for her editorial comments. I also want to thank my anonymous reviewers for their helpful comments on earlier drafts.

I'd like to thank my parents, who live thousands of miles away in Korea, where I was born and raised. Their understanding, kindness, and unfailing love have been my most fundamental support. I am very fortunate to have wonderful friends as well: in particular, D. C. Lee, who simply makes my life better and more fulfilling. Finally, I must make mention of the many immigrants I have encountered, who always inspire me to thrive.

Published online in Wiley Online Library
(wileyonlinelibrary.com) • DOI: 10.1002/aehe.20006

Introduction, Context, and Overview

THE UNITED STATES IS A COUNTRY of immigrants. It encompasses people from every corner of the world facing a vast range of circumstances and challenges, with more new immigrants arriving every day. Amid growing concerns about the economic recession, national security, and demographic shifts, important questions arise concerning immigrants in the United States (Suárez-Orozco, Yoshikawa, Teranishi, and Suárez-Orozco, 2011): What does it mean to be *American* in a multiethnic society? And can our nation provide these immigrants and their children with opportunities for upward mobility and positive prospects (Kasinitz, Mollenkopf, Waters, and Holdaway, 2008)?

Higher education, which serves as a pathway for immigrants to integrate into American society, has figured prominently in immigration reform debates. With many countries of origin, a wide geographic dispersion, and varying statuses of immigration, the diversity of the immigrant population, coupled with national and state immigration policies constantly in flux, poses a set of complex challenges to which higher education must respond (Fix and Passel, 2003). However, there is a scarcity of research informing a comprehensive understanding of the educational experiences and outcomes of immigrant students in higher education, with little knowledge available on demographic characteristics, postsecondary education enrollment patterns, overall college experiences, and educational attainment. Thus, immigrant students in higher education are underexamined, inaccurately characterized, and often misunderstood (Teranishi, Suárez-Orozco, and Suárez-Orozco, 2011).

According to the U.S. Census Bureau (2012), foreign-born population accounted for almost 13 percent of the entire U.S. population in 2010, compared with only 4.7 percent four decades ago. Increases in the size and diversity of the immigrant population have brought about a sweeping demographic change in the United States (Camarota, 2011; Passel and Cohn, 2012). As such, the future of the United States depends largely on whether or not the immigrant population succeeds in becoming an integral part of society. This transformation, in turn, depends on how well the nation's educational system prepares its immigrants to become productive citizens (Ordovensky and Hagy, 1998).

Why Focus on Immigrants?

While an accurate count of the national immigrant student population at the postsecondary education level is not available, based on data from the National Postsecondary Student Aid Study (NPSAS:08),[1] it was estimated that immigrants accounted for about 23 percent of all undergraduate students in 2007–2008: First-generation (foreign-born) immigrants and second-generation (U.S.-born with at least one foreign-born parent) immigrants accounted for 10 percent and 13 percent, respectively, of all undergraduate students in 2007–2008 (U.S. Department of Education, 2012b). Immigrant youth (including both U.S.-born youth with at least one immigrant parent and foreign-born youth who arrived in the United States by the age of twelve years) accounted for one out of six people aged eighteen to thirty-two years, and one-quarter of the U.S. population under the age of eighteen years in 2005 (U.S. Census Bureau, 2005). It is projected that immigrant students will represent almost 30 percent of the public school population by 2015 and will be of college age in the next decade (Fix and Passel, 2003). This rapid growth comes at a time when postsecondary education has never been more important for individual economic well-being and job security, as well as democratic citizenship. Understanding issues pertinent to the education of immigrant students in postsecondary institutions is particularly crucial because higher education prepares students to participate in the rapidly growing knowledge economy within the broader context of globalization (Suárez-Orozco, 2001).

The Immigration and Nationality Act of 1965 ended a quota system favoring European immigrants, and today's immigrants come from every part of the world, with newcomers from Latin America and Asia making up the majority. Unlike previous waves of immigrants, who sought to assimilate into the White, middle-class norms of their adopted country, immigrants today contribute to a wide landscape of racial, ethnic, and social class in the United States, giving rise to diversity in education at all levels.

In 1970, approximately 83 percent of the U.S. population were non-Hispanic Whites and only 6 percent were Hispanics or Asians; by 2009, 66 percent were non-Hispanic Whites and 19 percent were Hispanics and Asians taken together (Martin and Midgley, 2010). Both of these groups have increased by about 43 percent in the past decade, and together they have accounted for 71 percent of the U.S. population gain since 2000. If current trends continue, it is projected that the percentage of non-Hispanic Whites will decline to about 50 percent by 2050 while Hispanics and Asians will rise to one-third of the U.S. population (Martin and Midgley, 2010). According to the Pew Hispanic Center (2011), 82 percent of this projected increase will be attributable to immigration while only 18 percent of the U.S. population growth will be due to a natural increase of the baseline population. Paralleling to the national demographic trend, more than 90 percent of Asian and 66 percent of Hispanic undergraduates were immigrant-origin students (including both first- and second-generation immigrants) in 2007–2008 (U.S. Department of Education, 2012b). Given that racial and ethnic minorities are often at a socioeconomic disadvantage, the vast majority of recent immigrants who are non-White are more likely to encounter difficulties assimilating and adjusting to educational settings. Such barriers and discrimination are based not only on skin color but also on cultural attributes and the country of origin (Barker, 1981; Lee and Rice, 2007; Spears, 1999). Furthermore, recent immigrant students, who are more likely to be low-income and linguistically disadvantaged (Erisman and Looney, 2007), might face additional challenges balancing the value system of their home culture with American ideals (Harklau, 1998), which has a range of consequences for them and society (Perez, 2010). Yet policymakers, researchers, and pundits often overlook issues related to the educational experiences of immigrant college students. With this in mind, our intent is to synthesize the current body of research on immigrant students and lay a foundation for future research on the growing presence of the immigrant student population in higher education. In this volume, we will provide a context for understanding immigrants and higher education in the United States, offer a better understanding of the issues and conditions related to transition to college and progression through college, and suggest areas of future research to foster college access and success for this important but understudied population.

Immigrant as a Conceptual Term

Before we begin a review of existing literature on immigrant students in higher education, it is important to understand what we mean by *immigrant* and how the term has been operationalized in the existing literature. An immigrant is commonly defined as a foreign-born person who enters the United States with the intention to settle here permanently (Erisman and Looney, 2007). Although the term may initially appear straightforward, several variations in definition arise depending on nativity, legal residence, and generational status.

For the purposes of this monograph, the term *immigrant student* (also called *immigrant-origin student*) broadly refers to students who have moved to the United States from abroad at some point in their lives and (intend to) live here permanently *as well as* those who were born in the United States with at least one immigrant parent. The definition excludes temporary migrants (such as international students) because, by definition, they do not intend to reside in the United States permanently, although their intentions may change. The topic of temporary migrants, who we typically refer to as "international students," merits its own volume, and it is beyond the scope of this monograph. Though we have provided a clear definition of the term *immigrant,* readers should bear in mind that there is no uniform definition of *immigrant* employed by policymakers and educational researchers. Therefore, our aim is not to provide a singular way to define this term but to provide a conceptual overview to illuminate its complexity and suggest implications as to the term's use in higher education research and practice.

FIGURE 1

A Conceptual Model for the Multiple Dimensions of the Term *Immigrant*

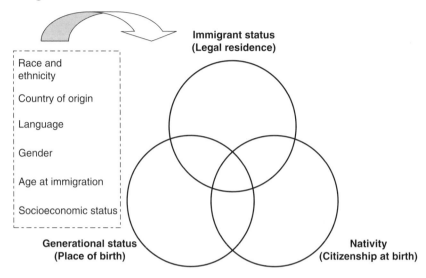

Our conceptual model intends to capture three core dimensions along which to define *immigrant:* (1) nativity (citizenship at birth), (2) legal residence, and (3) generational status (place of birth) (see Figure 1). This model is dynamic and subject to change, depending on which aspects of the immigrant group are considered for data collection and the focus of research. The intersecting circles depicted in the figure demonstrate that a definition of the term *immigrant* that uses one dimension can be understood in relation to the other dimensions—no one area may be understood to singularly describe what it means to be an immigrant. The dashed square illustrates that immigrant groups are markedly heterogeneous, varying greatly in race and ethnicity, country of origin, age at immigration, language, gender, and socio-economic background—all factors that profoundly impact the processes and outcomes of adaptation to a host country, such as educational attainment and workforce participation.

The nativity of immigrants is determined by citizenship at birth with two distinct subcategories: native-born and foreign-born. According to the U.S.

Census Bureau (2012), native-born means all those who are born either in the United States or abroad to U.S. citizen parents; the foreign-born population is all persons who are not U.S. citizens at birth, including naturalized U.S. citizens, legal permanent residents, temporary migrants (such as foreign students), humanitarian migrants (such as refugees), and illegal immigrants. Unfortunately, the U.S. Census Bureau provides information on the aggregate total foreign-born population without disaggregating the data by immigrant status.

Immigrant status (legal residence) distinguishes immigrants from nonimmigrants based on whether foreign-born persons (intend to) establish permanent residence in the United States. The Office of Immigration Statistics (OIS), a division of the U.S. Department of Homeland Security, collects annual data on the foreign-born population by immigrant status: immigrants and nonimmigrants (or nonpermanent residents). Immigrants are defined by this office as foreign-born persons who (intend to) *live permanently* in the United States, while nonimmigrants are those foreign-born who reside in the United States *temporarily*. When using immigrant status to define the term *immigrant,* we include naturalized citizens, legal residents (legal permanent residents, refugees, and asylees), and unauthorized immigrants. Temporary migrants (for example, international students) are included in the nonimmigrant category.

Another federal agency, the National Center for Education Statistics (NCES), part of the U.S. Department of Education, also collects data on immigrants through the Integrated Postsecondary Education Data System (IPEDS), looking at two subcategories of legal residence: resident aliens versus nonresident aliens. A resident alien refers to a person who is not a U.S. citizen (either at birth or naturalized) but who has been admitted as a legal resident for the purpose of obtaining permanent residence in the United States; nonresident alien refers to someone who is not a U.S. citizen and who resides in the United States on a visa or temporary basis and does not have the right to remain permanently. The data, however, make no distinction between naturalized citizens (foreign-born) and those who are citizens from birth because at least one parent in these groups is a U.S. citizen and lumps the two groups into the foreign-born citizen category. The U.S. Department of Education data sometimes include undocumented immigrants, usually including them in the foreign (international) student category.

Our model also looks at generational status or whether one individual or his/her parent(s) were born outside the United States. This dimension concerns the birthplace of a person as well as that of his or her parents. A first-generation immigrant is foreign-born and immigrated after birth; a second-generation immigrant was born in the United States to at least one foreign-born parent. The first- and second-generation are often grouped together as immigrant groups and referred to as immigrant-origin. A third- or higher generation is considered to be a native generation—both individual and parents were born in the United States (see, for example, Jensen, 2001; Kao and Tienda, 1995). Studies of immigrants by generational status have drawn considerable attention from educational researchers, primarily due to growing disparities in educational achievement and the degree to which generations differ in assimilation into educational settings.

Bearing these three dimensions in mind, we must be careful to remember that an immigrant defined in one context might not be labeled as such in another, and the terms used to define the word *immigrant* used in one circumstance might be quite different in another.

Definitions of Key Terms

Before we begin a brief discussion of the U.S. immigration context and demographic trends, it is necessary to establish a common understanding of several key terms pertaining to any discussion of immigrants.

- *Native-born* includes anyone who was a U.S. citizen at birth, including persons born in the United States, Puerto Rico, a U.S. Island Area (U.S. Virgin Islands, Guam, American Samoa, or the Commonwealth of the Northern Mariana Islands), or abroad of a U.S. citizen parent or parents (Gryn and Larsen, 2010).
- *Foreign-born* includes persons who were not U.S. citizens at birth, such as those who have become U.S. citizens through naturalization and legal permanent residents, temporary migrants (for example, foreign students), humanitarian migrants (for example, refugees), and undocumented immigrants (people residing in the United States without legal authorization)

(Gryn and Larsen, 2010). This term excludes those born in a foreign country to American citizens.

- *Legal resident immigrant population* is defined as all foreign-born persons who are granted lawful residence—legal permanent residents (LPRs), naturalized citizens, asylees, refugees, and nonimmigrants for a temporary stay in the United States. It excludes those who are foreign-born to U.S. citizens.

- *Naturalized citizens* are all foreign-born persons who have become U.S. citizens after fulfilling the citizenship requirements, including residing in the United States for at least five years after obtaining permanent residency and demonstrating proficiency in English, knowledge of U.S. history and government, and good moral character (Simanski and Rytina, 2006). Naturalization is the process by which U.S. citizenship is conferred upon foreign citizens or nationals after fulfilling the requirements established by Congress in the Immigration and Nationality Act (INA). After naturalization, foreign-born citizens enjoy all the same benefits, rights, and responsibilities that the Constitution gives to native-born U.S. citizens, including the right to vote (U.S. Department of Homeland Security, www.dhs.gov /files/statistics/publications/gc_1302103955524.shtm).

- *Legal permanent residents* (so-called "green card" holders) are the foreign-born who have been granted the right to live permanently in the United States (Jefferys and Rytina, 2006).

- *Undocumented (illegal or unauthorized) immigrants* are foreign-born nationals who enter the United States, often with the intention of remaining there, without legal status, or who stay beyond the authorized period after their legal entry, or who violate their terms of legal entry. The terms *undocumented, illegal,* and *unauthorized* are used interchangeably in this monograph[2]; *undocumented immigrant students* are individuals who were brought to the United States by their parents without legal status and who are currently enrolled in an educational institution in the United States.

- *Temporary residents or nonresident aliens* (also called *nonimmigrants*) are the foreign-born who enter the United States on a temporary basis for a specified length of time, including tourists, business travelers, foreign students, temporary workers, and diplomats (Grieco, 2006). The term *nonimmigrant* is sometimes used to refer to native-born counterparts in social science and educational research.

- *International (foreign) students* are defined as individuals who are enrolled for credit at an accredited higher education institution in the United States on a temporary visa, and who are not immigrants (permanent residents), undocumented immigrants, or refugees.

- *Migrant students* are defined as students from families that move around between the United States and other countries to pursue seasonal employment opportunities.

- *Humanitarian migrants* refer to a special group of foreign legal residents including *refugees* and *asylees*. According to the Immigration and Nationality Act (INA), a refugee is defined as a person who is unable or unwilling to return to his or her country of nationality because of persecution or a well-founded fear of persecution on account of race, religion, nationality, membership in a particular social group, or political opinion. Refugees apply for admission to the Immigration and Naturalization Service outside the United States. *Asylees*, however, seek protection within the United States or at a port of entry. Refugees and asylees are generally admitted to the United States as nonimmigrants. Refugees enter the country legally and often with the intention of remaining permanently but are required to wait one year before applying for official immigrant status (Martin, 2011).

- *First-generation immigrants* refer to foreign-born nationals who enter the United States for permanent residency. Some scholars distinguish first-generation (those who immigrated at age eighteen years or older) and 1.5 generation (those who immigrated as school-age children (Rumbaut and Ima, 1988). Even so, depending on the age of arrival, some authors make an even finer distinction by dividing immigrants into 1.25, 1.5, and 1.75 generations. For example, the 1.25 generation consists of those who enter the United States between age thirteen and seventeen years, 1.5 generation immigrants come to the United States between age seven and twelve years, and those in the 1.75 generation immigrate to the United States as preschoolers (between age zero and six years) (Rumbaut, 2007).

- *Second-generation immigrants* (often called children from immigrant families) refer to the U.S.-born with one or both foreign-born parents. Some authors also distinguish 2.5 generation immigrants (U.S.-born with only one immigrant parent) from second-generation immigrants (U.S.-born with two immigrant parents) (DebBurman, 2005).
- *The third or higher generations* are those who are U.S.-born with at least one second-generation immigrant parent.

Limitations of the Monograph

There are a few key limitations to this monograph that should be explicitly acknowledged here. At the outset, we defined *immigrants* as foreign nationals who enter the United States with the intent to reside here permanently, as well as those individuals who are U.S.-born with at least one immigrant parent. Therefore, our immigrant population of primary interest combines nativity, immigrant status, and generational status. In terms of nativity, we used the subcategory of those who are foreign-born to denote immigrant. As far as immigrant status is concerned, we exclude research on temporary and humanitarian migrants from this monograph, and with regard to generational status, we include both first- and second-generation immigrants in our review of the literature. However, though we include second-generation immigrant students in our discussion, many studies often do not distinguish first-generation immigrant students from second-generation students, or second-generation immigrant students are often indiscriminately lumped in with native-born Americans; the term *immigrant* is not clearly defined altogether. Social scientists and educational researchers often use the terms *immigrant youth*, *children of immigrants*, or *students in immigrant families*, combining both first-and second-generation immigrants in their research.

We also acknowledge the heterogeneity of the wider immigrant population. Our attempt here is not to describe the immigrant population monolithically. However, due to space constraints, it is nearly impossible to discuss the range of experiences among diverse groups of immigrant students, so our goal is to comprehensively synthesize the existing knowledge base on immigrants in higher education and provide an initial point for the higher education community to become aware of issues and policies surrounding this emerging student population.

Organization of the Monograph

This monograph reviews and synthesizes literature that addresses the overall educational experiences of immigrant students in higher education, with special attention to access to and persistence in college for this growing student population. While we know a lot about the increasing number of immigrants who go to college, we know considerably less about those who are actually transitioning to college, and what obstacles they face with regard to attendance and overall collegiate experience. In this monograph, we attempt to provide a baseline understanding of such challenges, as well as a theoretical lens for understanding the educational experiences of immigrant student groups at the postsecondary education level, and insights into ways in which the higher education community can better serve these students in order to improve their quality of education and eventual academic and career goals. In addition, questions are posed as to how—and how well—colleges and universities have responded to the growing immigrant population on campus. The picture that emerges is largely one of inattention, coupled with widespread assumptions about immigrant students. These assumptions, which are unconfirmed by empirical data and research, could result in unfair practices, as well as reduced educational quality for a diverse immigrant student body. Because of higher education's critical role in promoting social and economic mobility, the academic community needs to focus more attention on issues related to these students.

In the following chapter, we introduce key theoretical frameworks and concepts that are useful in framing the overall educational experiences of the immigrant student population. We then turn to major factors that influence access to college for various immigrant student subgroups, followed by a chapter that provides a discussion synthesizing literature related to a range of aspects of immigrant students' educational experiences while attending college. In the fifth chapter, entitled "Undocumented Students and Higher Education," we focus specifically on a distinctive immigrant student subpopulation: undocumented students, and some of the unique challenges faced by them. This subtopic is particularly timely as recent immigration issues have become sociopolitically divisive and immigration reform policy at the state and federal level is constantly challenged. In the sixth chapter, we discuss the indispensable role that community colleges play as a gateway to postsecondary education for diverse immigrant populations and present examples of a number of initiatives to educate immigrant students across community college campuses. The final chapter suggests directions for future research and implications for policy and practice to fill existing knowledge gaps in order to better serve the needs of immigrant students while successfully making the transition to and through college.

A Context for Immigration in the United States

We present information on recent demographic trends in immigrants' educational attainment and participation in the U.S. workforce to provide a context for our discussion of immigrant-origin students in higher education. This information is derived from data collected by the U.S. Census Bureau and the Department of Homeland Security (DHS). The U.S. Census data sources used in this section often do not disaggregate the immigrant population by some of the categories we introduced earlier, such as immigrant status. As a result, the data are based primarily on citizenship at birth (native-born versus foreign-born). *Foreign-born* and *immigrant* are used interchangeably here, both referring to all persons who were born outside the United States and are residents of the United States, except for those born abroad to U.S. citizens.

One of the salient features of recent immigrant groups is their diversity of language, country of origin, socioeconomic circumstance, and pattern of immigration (Zhou, 1997). Immigrants who came to the United States prior to 1965 had education levels similar to those of native-born Americans and earned wages that were, on average, higher than those of native-born employees. Since the mid-1960s, however, the education levels of new immigrants have fallen behind those of native-born Americans, resulting in the average wages of immigrants falling well below those of the native population as well (Rector, 2006). As a result, recent immigrants increasingly occupy the low end of the U.S. socioeconomic spectrum. Another characteristic of recent immigrants is that they tend to be more concentrated in large metropolitan areas than the native-born, with 85 percent of immigrants living in the 100 largest metros in 2009 (Suro, Wilson, and Singer, 2011). Though the immigrant population continues to grow in those gateways, many immigrants now settle in suburban areas, accounting for 30 percent of the overall population growth in the suburbs from 2000 to 2009 (Suro, Wilson, and Singer, 2011). Coupled with their increasingly large numbers, the rapid influx of immigrants with many different languages and cultures will bring about significant educational, social, cultural, and political transformations in American society.

Until the 1960s, immigrants were predominantly from European countries. The post-1965 immigration era has witnessed significant waves of immigration into the United States, with a large-scale immigration from Latin and Asian countries occurring in the past four decades and continuing well into the twenty-first century.[3] According to the U.S. Census Bureau's 2010 American Community Survey, the immigrant population in the United States was estimated at 39.9 million, with approximately 1.5 million new immigrants arriving every year (Passel and Cohn, 2012); this means that approximately one in eight U.S. residents is foreign-born. Between 2005 and 2050, the U.S. population is projected to increase by 48 percent, with the immigrant population projected to account for 82 percent of that growth. In particular, Hispanics will make up 29 percent of the total U.S. population by 2050, compared with 14 percent in 2005 (Passel and Cohn, 2008).

In 2010, the largest share of the foreign-born U.S. population came from Latin America, comprising 54.2 percent of the immigrant population, followed by Asia (27 percent), and Europe (12 percent) (see Figure 2). The foreign-born population from Mexico accounted for 29.4 percent (11.7 million) of the total foreign-born population followed by China (5 percent) with India and the Philippines each representing approximately 4 percent of the immigrant population (Batalova and Lee, 2012). Vietnam, El Salvador, Cuba, and Korea comprised about 2 percent each. Within the foreign-born population from Latin America, Mexican immigrants comprised 56 percent, followed by Caribbean (17.8 percent), Central American (14.6 percent), and South American immigrants (11.6 percent). In terms of race and ethnicity,

FIGURE 2
Immigrant Population in the United States by Country of Origin

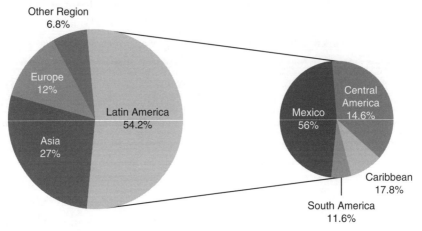

Source: U.S. Census Bureau, American Community Survey, 2010.

47.1 percent of foreign-born population reported their race/ethnicity as Hispanic, 7.6 percent as Black, 24.3 percent as Asian, and 18.7 percent as non-Hispanic White (Patten, 2012). Of the almost 40 million foreign-born in the U.S., women accounted for about 51 percent in 2010 (Batalova and Lee, 2012). Although the immigrant population resides in all states, they tend to be more concentrated in some states. In 2010, immigrants accounted for more than 20 percent of the population in California (10.1 million, 27.2 percent), New York (4.2 million, 22.2 percent), and New Jersey (1.8 million, 21 percent), and close to 20 percent of the population in Florida (3.6 million, 19.4 percent) and Nevada (more than half a million, 18.8 percent) (Camarota, 2011).

About two in five (17.5 million) foreign-born residents in the United States were naturalized citizens, compared with 56 percent (22.5 million) in 2010 (Batalova and Lee, 2012). With regard to citizenship status, there were considerable variations by region of origin. For example, over 55 percent of the foreign-born from Asia and Europe were naturalized citizens, compared with 32 percent of the foreign-born from Latin America including Mexico and other Central American countries, indicating varying rates of naturalization on a demographic and legal basis (Gryn and Larsen, 2010).[4]

Educational Attainment of Immigrants

Overall, the foreign-born population has relatively lower educational attainment than the U.S.-born population as a whole. Although the proportion of immigrants with advanced degrees (10.1 percent) and those with a high school degree or less (62.5 percent) in 2005 has stayed approximately the same as that before 1970, the percent of immigrants with a bachelor's degree has increased from 12.7 percent before 1970 to 22.2 percent in 2005 (Haskins, 2007). As shown in Figure 3, more than one-fifth of foreign-born residents had less than a ninth grade education, compared with only 3.3 percent of the native-born population. Forty-one percent of the foreign-born population age twenty-five years and older received a high school diploma or some college education compared with 60.6 percent of the native-born.

In contrast, the percentage of college graduates in the immigrant population (15.9 percent) was slightly lower than that of the native-born (18.1 percent) and 27 percent of foreign-born age twenty-five years and older had a bachelor's degree or higher compared with a similarly close 28.4 percent of the native-born, indicating only a slightly higher attainment level for the native-born population. Also, the percentages of foreign-born and native-born who had an advanced degree were roughly the same (11.1 percent and 10.3 percent respectively). However, the percentage of foreign-born adults ages twenty-five years and older who had some college education was far lower (18.8 percent) than that of native-born adults (30.9 percent).

As shown in Figure 4, there are both similarities and differences in the level of educational attainment of the foreign-born population age twenty-five years and older, depending on region of origin. Across the regions, more than 20 percent of the foreign-born population completed a high school diploma (27.3 percent for European immigrants, 21.1 percent for Asian immigrants, 27.7 percent for Latin American immigrants, and 22.8 percent for immigrants from other areas). Asian immigrants had the highest percentage of completion of bachelor's degree (31.6 percent), followed by European immigrants (24.8 percent), immigrants from other areas (22.4 percent), and

FIGURE 3
Educational Attainment Rates of the Population Twenty-Five Years and Older by Nativity 2010

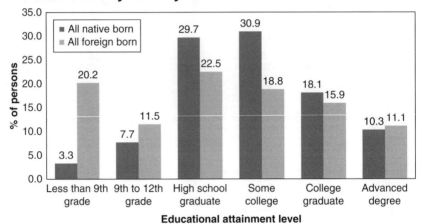

Source: Pew Hispanic Center (2011).

FIGURE 4
Educational Attainment of Immigrants Twenty-Five Years and Older by Region of Country, 2010

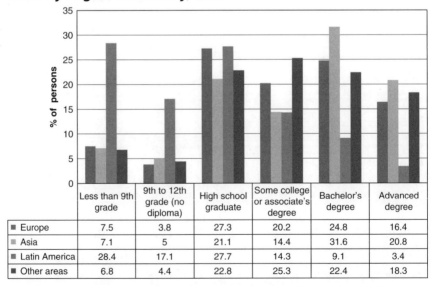

	Less than 9th grade	9th to 12th grade (no diploma)	High school graduate	Some college or associate's degree	Bachelor's degree	Advanced degree
■ Europe	7.5	3.8	27.3	20.2	24.8	16.4
■ Asia	7.1	5	21.1	14.4	31.6	20.8
■ Latin America	28.4	17.1	27.7	14.3	9.1	3.4
■ Other areas	6.8	4.4	22.8	25.3	22.4	18.3

Source: U.S. Census Bureau, the Current Population Survey, 2010, "Annual Social and Economic Supplement," www.census.gov/population/www/socdemo/foreign/datatlbs.html.

immigrants from Latin America (9.1 percent). The percentage of immigrants who did not receive a high school diploma was virtually the same for immigrants from Europe, Asia, and other areas (12 percent to 13 percent each), whereas the majority (45.5 percent) of immigrants from Latin America did not receive a high school diploma.

Foreign-born youth contribute significantly to the high school dropout rate in the United States. According to the Pew Hispanic Center (Patten, 2012), the high school dropout rate for the foreign-born population from sixteen to nineteen years of age was 11 percent in 2010, down from 23.4 percent in 2000, compared with 4.5 percent of the native-born population, down from 8.5 percent in 2000. Of the foreign-born population who dropped out of high school, Central American immigrants comprised the largest proportion (25.4 percent), followed by those from Mexico (21 percent), the Caribbean (7.7 percent), and the Middle East (4.8 percent), while the high school dropout rate for the foreign-born immigrants from Asia was roughly 2 percent (Patten, 2012).

As shown in Table 1, overall college enrollment for the traditional college-age foreign-born cohort (ages eighteen to twenty-four years) was lower (35.1 percent) than that of the native-born (43.9 percent) in 2010 (Patten, 2012). However, there was little difference in college enrollment rates between foreign-born adults age twenty-five years and older and their native-born counterparts (5 percent and 4.9 percent, respectively). Immigrants of eighteen to twenty-four years showed considerable variation in college enrollment rates by region of origin: 64.2 percent of immigrants from South and East Asia were enrolled in some form of postsecondary education, followed by 57.5 percent of immigrants from the Middle East, 55.7 percent of immigrants from all other areas, 44 percent of South American immigrants, and 37.2 percent of Caribbean immigrants. Immigrants from Mexico had the lowest college enrollment rate, 12.3 percent. Immigrants' postsecondary enrollment rates also vary by their length of residence in the country. According to Erisman and Looney (2007), only 22 percent of immigrants between the ages of eighteen and twenty-four years who came to the United States between the ages of thirteen and nineteen years were enrolled in college, compared with 37 percent of those who arrived before the age of thirteen years (Erisman and Looney, 2007).

TABLE 1
College Enrollment of the Foreign-Born Population by Nativity and Country of Origin: 2010

	Ages Eighteen Through Twenty-Four Years		Ages Twenty-Five Years and Older	
	Number Enrolled in College	Enrollment Rate (%)	Number Enrolled in College	Enrollment Rate (%)
All native-born	12,307,432	43.9	8,374,676	4.9
All foreign-born	1,218,420	35.1	1,679,785	5.0
Mexico	159,351	12.3	207,149	2.2
Asia	480,779	64.2	554,002	6.5
Caribbean	103,026	37.2	185,702	5.7
Central America	103,634	44.0	78,270	3.1
South America	81,412	38.5	161,660	7.0
Middle East	58,154	57.5	107,253	8.9
All other	272,704	55.7	385,749	6.1

Source: Pew Hispanic Center (2011).

Previous research has shown mixed results as to the effect of generational status on academic performance among immigrant students. For example, Portes and Rumbaut (2001) found that the grade-point averages of second-generation immigrants tend to drop as they live longer in the United States. However, first-generation students are more likely to drop out of high school than those in the second or third generation (Perreira, Harris, and Lee, 2006). As shown in Table 2, almost 30 percent of first-generation immigrants did not complete a high school education, compared to only 11.5 percent of second-generation immigrants. Upward educational progress has been noted in subsequent generations, in terms of the percentage who completed high school and those who had some college, up to an associate's degree. However, this pattern did not persist from second to third generation for those who completed a college or graduate degree. For example, 25.5 percent of first-generation immigrants completed a high school education, compared with 28.8 percent of second-generation and 32.7 percent of third and higher generations. However, 19.5 percent of third and higher generations completed a bachelor's degree, higher than the 18.1 percent of first-generation immigrants but lower than the 21.3 percent of second-generation immigrants (U.S. Census Bureau, 2010).

These differences in educational attainment become more pronounced among immigrants by citizenship status. Among nonnaturalized immigrants, only 22 percent had attended at least some college, whereas, among naturalized citizens, those with some attendance were as high as 41 percent (Erisman and Looney, 2007). Furthermore, almost half (46 percent) of immigrants who migrated to the United States between the ages of thirteen and nineteen years are more likely to be at a disadvantage in educational attainment. In this group, 21 percent had attended at least some college, compared with 34 percent of immigrants who came to the United States before the age of thirteen years.

The effects of generational status on postsecondary enrollment and educational attainment vary by race and ethnicity. The analysis of the NPSAS:08 indicates that more than half of all Asian undergraduates were foreign-born, first-generation immigrants (55 percent), compared with 21 percent of Hispanic and 10 percent of Black immigrant undergraduates in 2007–2008. Conversely, the large proportion of Hispanic undergraduates was primarily second-generation immigrants (45 percent), while 38 percent of Asian and

TABLE 2
Educational Attainment of Immigrants Twenty-Five Years and Older by Generation, 2010 (in Percent)

| | Generation | | | |
| | | | Third and | |
Educational Attainment	First	Second	Later	Total
Less than ninth grade	18.5	4.1	2.6	5.2
Ninth to twelfth grade (no diploma)	11.3	7.4	6.9	7.7
High school graduate	25.5	28.8	32.7	31.2
Some college or associate's degree	15.8	25.6	28.1	26.0
Bachelor's degree	18.1	21.3	19.5	19.4
Master's degree/professional degree	8.8	11.0	9.0	9.1
Doctorate degree	2.0	1.8	1.2	1.4
Total	100	100	100	100

Source: U.S. Census Bureau (2010).

7 percent of Black undergraduates are second-generation. Among first-generation immigrant undergraduate students, Asians accounted for 30 percent, followed by Hispanics at 26 percent, Whites at 24 percent, and 15 percent Black immigrants at 15 percent. Among second-generation immigrant students, Hispanics accounted for 41 percent of all second-generation immigrant undergraduates, with the rest made up of 28 percent White, 16 percent Asian, and 7 percent Black (U.S. Department of Education, 2012b). Using the U.S. Census Bureau's Current Population Survey of March 2009, Baum and Flores (2011) reported that 30 percent of Black first-generation immigrants received a college degree or higher, compared with 42 percent of their second-generation Black counterparts and 18 percent of third or higher generations. In contrast, both Asian (two-thirds) and White (more than half) first-generation immigrants earned at least a bachelor's degree. However, only 9 percent of Hispanic first-generation immigrants completed a bachelor's degree or higher compared with second and later generations (19 percent for second-generation and 16 percent for third- or higher generation).

Employment of Immigrants in the United States

Immigrants are a fast-growing segment of the U.S. labor market. During the past decade, foreign-born workers accounted for more than half of the growth of the U.S. workforce (Alsalam and Smith, 2005). In 2010, Hispanic immigrants accounted for 49.9 percent of the immigrant workforce in the U.S., followed by Asians (21.8 percent). According to the U.S. Bureau of Labor Statistics (2011), immigrants made up 15.8 percent of the labor force in 2010: the sheer number of foreign-born immigrant workers (age sixteen years and older) increased from 23,926,000 in 2009 to 24,356,000 in 2010, while the number of native-born workers decreased from 154,142,000 to 153,889,000 in 2010. Immigrants hold a disproportionately large share of jobs that require very little formal education. In 2010, among workers age twenty-five years and older who lacked a high school diploma, nearly half were foreign-born, and most of those were from Mexico and Central America (U.S. Bureau of Labor Statistics, 2011). Although immigrant workers can be found in virtually every occupation and industry, they are concentrated in low-skill occupations in construction, cleaning and maintenance, and restaurants. This is particularly true for recent immigrants from Latin America (Alsalam and Smith, 2005). Breaking down the immigrant labor force occupationally, we find that 28 percent of immigrants are in management, professional, and related occupations; 25 percent in service occupations; 17.3 percent in sales and office occupations; 13.6 percent in natural resources, construction, and maintenance occupations; and 16.1 percent in production, transportation, and material-moving occupations (U.S. Bureau of Labor Statistics, 2011).

According to the U.S. Bureau of Labor Statistics (2011), 26.5 percent of foreign-born workers age twenty-five years and older did not complete high school, compared with 5.4 percent of their native-born counterparts, indicating lower educational attainment for foreign-born workers on the high school level in 2010. The educational attainment gap does shrink at the postsecondary level. For example, 31.1 percent of foreign-born workers age twenty-five years and older had completed college or an advanced degree, compared with 35.3 percent of those native-born workers. While 29.9 percent of native-born workers attended some college or completed an associate's degree, only 17.1 percent of foreign-born workers did so (U.S. Bureau of Labor Statistics, 2011).

Immigrants accounted for 15 percent of the entire U.S. college-educated labor force in 2007 (Batalova and Fix, 2008). However, they tend to be concentrated in certain occupations: Immigrants represent nearly 27 percent of physicians, over 34 percent of computer software engineers, and over 42 percent of medical scientists. Almost three-quarters of the foreign-born, college-educated labor force were Asian and non-Hispanic White, while about 18 percent of college-educated immigrants were of Latin origin (Batalova and Fix, 2008). More than 1.3 million college-educated immigrants in the United States are unemployed or working unskilled jobs well below their level of education and competency (Batalova and Fix, 2008).

The earning rates of foreign-born workers are not as closely linked with their educational attainment as are those for native-born workers (Haskins, 2007). The median weekly earnings of foreign-born full-time workers were $598, compared with $771 for their native-born counterparts. With regard to the difference in wages by generational status, first-generation immigrants earned 20 percent less than native-born workers of a similar age, whereas second-generation immigrant workers continue to earn wages that were 6.3 percent higher than the native-born Americans, indicating generational differences in the labor market (Haskins, 2007).

With the rising immigrant population in the United States over the past forty years, the extent to which immigrants are able to successfully participate in education and the workforce has become a critical societal issue. As many studies have suggested a positive association between college education and socioeconomic gains and stability, many immigrant students and their families regard postsecondary education as a gateway to upward social and economic mobility. However, the foreign-born population's educational attainment and labor market participation are relatively lower than those of the native-born population. More important, to a considerable extent, educational attainment and employment vary by race/ethnicity, generation status, and immigrant status. Thus, it is important to make it clear that the educational and occupational outcomes of immigrants can be understood by looking at a complex socioeconomic landscape that includes not only demographic considerations but also the population's heterogeneity within.

In the next chapter, we discuss key theoretical frameworks and conceptual approaches for the study of the educational experiences of the immigrant student population, including neo-racism theory, social-ecological perspectives, acculturation and assimilation theories, and social capital theory.

Theoretical Foundation: Immigrant Student College Transition and Persistence

UNDERSTANDING ISSUES RELATED TO EDUCATING immigrant students, whether they are first- or second-generation, legal or unauthorized, is critically important to the future of the United States. Large-scale waves of new immigration from Latin America, Asia, and the Caribbean have caused the immigrant population to increase and diversify over the past four decades (Oh and Cooc, 2011). Though limited research is available, national estimates do show that more than one out of five students enrolled in U.S. postsecondary institutions in 2007–2008 came from immigrant backgrounds (U.S. Department of Education, 2012b). Despite the growing presence of immigrant students in the American higher education landscape, there is a lack of empirical research on how immigrant students navigate transitions to college, psychosocial adjustment, cultural values, and academic and social engagement, all factors that influence college persistence and success. We believe building theoretical underpinnings that adequately explore the multiplicity of diverse immigrant students' experiences and contexts is necessary to the development and implementation of effective policy, practice, and research in higher education. In this chapter, we draw upon multiple disciplinary traditions, such as psychology, sociology, political science, and education, to provide conceptual frameworks to guide research in this area, examining the educational experiences of immigrant-origin students and the varied dimensions of life that shape their college transition and educational experiences. Such frameworks include neo-racism theory, social-ecological perspectives, acculturation and assimilation theories, and social capital theory.

Neo-Racism

What it means to be American is constantly evolving, and the national culture is extremely heterogeneous. As a nation of immigrants, the United States rests on a multicultural foundation. No single pattern has defined who is an American, and constant immigration causes American identity to continuously evolve (De la Garza, Falcon, and Garcia, 1996; Fraga and Segura, 2006). However, recent debates on immigration reform and discussions of the recent surge of Asian and Latin American immigrants have raised concerns as to threats to national security, disintegration of traditional American values, and demographic balkanization, where a geographically and culturally segmented population exists as a consequence of immigration (Frey, 1995, 1996; Schlesinger, 1992), intensified by precarious economic conditions such as high unemployment rates and a shrinking middle class. These sentiments appear to rest on a sense of the importance of a unified national culture preserving democratic, "American" ideals, and view cultural pluralism as a threat to American values. As anti-immigration sentiments have become more visible over the past decade, the term *neo-racism,* or "new racism," has played an increasing role in shaping some public attitudes toward immigrants in the United States.

Neo-racism refers to forms of discrimination based not only on race/ethnicity but also on cultural and linguistic boundaries and national origin (Barker, 1981; Lee and Rice, 2007; Spears, 1999). According to Barker (1981), new racism is a form of racism not explicitly based on the perceived biological inferiority of groups in relation to one another, but rather on the incompatibility of the cultures, customs, and traditions of such groups. In other words, "neo-racism does not replace biological racism, but rather masks it by encouraging exclusion based on the cultural attributes or national origin of the oppressed" (Lee and Rice, 2007, p. 389). This new racism has arisen as increasing numbers of immigrants with different cultures and traditions traverse the country, leading to conflict and fears that cultural differences may threaten native identity. In the context of higher education, neo-racism can be manifested in admissions denial, unfair academic evaluations, inaccessibility or lack of access to financial aid, faculty or peer students' misperceptions of immigrants, or social obstacles to the formation of meaningful interpersonal relationships (Lee and Rice, 2007). Neo-racism is a useful framework to describe any form of discrimination encountered by immigrant students while transitioning into and passing through college.

Social-Ecological Model

The ecological systems theory, developed by Urie Bronfenbrenner, provides a conceptual framework for us to understand the influence of the environment on the educational outcomes and adaptation of immigrant students. Ecological systems theory is relevant to immigrant students because the model provides a theoretical lens through which reciprocal interactions between individuals and their environments are examined in the context of specific aspects of a student's life history, social and historical circumstances, culture, and time (Bronfenbrenner and Morris, 2006; Renn and Arnold, 2003; Serdarevic and Chronister, 2005). Two underlying "axioms" of Bronfenbrenner's (1993) theory make it theoretically and practically important: (1) "development is an evolving function of person-environment interaction" and (b) "ultimately, this interaction must take place in the immediate, face-to-face setting in which the person exists" (p. 10). Bronfenbrenner's (1993) social-ecological framework emphasizes the context-specific interaction between a person and their environment that "emerges as the most likely to exert influence on the course and content of subsequent psychological developments in all spheres" (p. 10). Basing his work on human developmental psychology, Bronfenbrenner (1979) proposed a four-component model: Process-Person-Context-Time (PPCT). Process refers to the interaction between the individual and the environment. The attributes of the person or individual that are most likely to shape development, for better or worse, are those that promote or hinder dynamic character in relation to the environment. Context is the most critical of the four components. Time refers to the sequence of events in a person's life, such as marriage, migration, or birth of a sibling, and can affect individuals differently, thus uniquely shaping a student's characteristics (Evans and others, 2010; Renn and Arnold, 2003). Time is crucial as it interacts with the other three components of process, person, and context, to affect the developmental processes (Evans and others, 2010).

In Bronfenbrenner's (1993) model, the person exists at the center of a complex environment, surrounded by four levels of context. These are the microsystem, mesosystem, exosystem, and macrosystem. Development occurs within each of these systems as well as between them.

According to Bronfenbrenner (1993), the microsystem is the most basic unit of analysis, consisting of the patterns of activities, roles, and interpersonal relationships that are experienced by a person in a given face-to-face setting. Setting, in this definition, is a place where people interact; roles refer to expected actions on the level of the individual as well as that of wider society; activities reference what people are doing; interpersonal relationships are how people treat each other when they are together (Poch, 2005). For example, college-peer microsystems are unique to immigrant students within the college-peer culture (Kim, 2008), so much so that even individuals within the same classroom will interact differently within that microsystem depending on their experiences (Renn and Arnold, 2003). The interactions between these microsystems can also influence the actions of a student within the current setting (Poch, 2005).

The mesosystem comprises links and processes between two or more settings in which a person actively participates (Bronfenbrenner, 1993; Poch, 2005). This system can be formed or expanded when a person moves, either physically or psychologically, to a new setting, or through other interconnections such as social networking, or formal and informal communications (Poch, 2005).

The exosystem is one or more settings not containing the individual as an active participant but still influencing the development of that individual (Renn and Arnold, 2003; Poch, 2005). Some examples of immigrant student exosystems include a parent's workplace, federal or state aid policies and institutional policies.

The final component of context in Bronfenbrenner's model is the macrosystem. This is the larger system in which the other three are nested. The macrosystem typically provides an overall framework for a person's developmental capabilities, yet exerts the most distant influence (Poch, 2005; Renn and Arnold, 2003). It is time and place dependent, and specific to a given culture at a particular moment in history (Poch, 2005).

FIGURE 5
A Social-Ecological Model for Immigrant Students

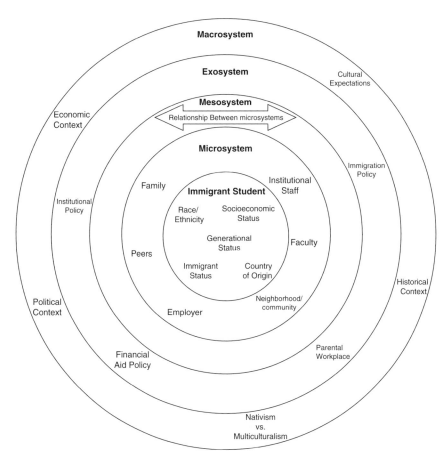

Figure 5 demonstrates the social-ecological model for immigrant students, showing that for this population, ecological systems consist of (1) microsystems (including family, peers, faculty, employer, institutional staff, neighborhood/community), (2) mesosystems (relationships between microsystems), (3) exosystems (parental workplace, financial aid policy, institutional policy, immigration policy), and (4) macrosystems (social, economic, and historical trends and contexts, cultural expectation, social forces—nativism versus multiculturalism). These systems are interrelated, nested, dynamic structures ranging from the immediate face-to-face settings to broader social contexts

(Bronfenbrenner and Morris, 2006). By taking into account the multiple factors that affect educational outcomes of immigrant students, this social-ecological framework is helpful in examining how immigrant students' interaction with these environments constrains or aids educational experiences. The social-ecological perspective is also useful for framing the family, neighborhood, and institutional challenges facing immigrant students and for understanding student-level characteristics as well as socio-cultural contexts that impede or enhance educational outcomes.

Acculturation and Assimilation Theories

When individuals decide to immigrate, their subsequent relocation may follow a patterned process. Sluzki (1979) has proposed that the process of immigration be viewed as a multistage one, including the following phases: (1) preparatory, (2) the act of immigration, (3) period of overcompensation, (4) decompensation or crisis, and (5) period of transgenerational impact. During the preparatory stage, the family begins planning, making decisions, and taking time to say goodbye to friends and relatives. The immigration stage, according to Sluzki, is experienced differently based on each family's access to legal documentation or economic resources. Consequently, a family with low socioeconomic status and no legal documentation can experience greater challenges in coming to the new country. The overcompensation stage is characterized by a strong desire to preserve cultural traditions and values from the country of origin. Maintaining these traditions and values allows the family to develop a sense of stability. Sluzki indicates that this stage may be a reaction to the changes in the family's surroundings and culture. In the decompensation or crisis stage, the family usually experiences conflict, often associated with acculturation and/or gender roles. Finally, in the period of transgenerational impact, the family continues to experience changes in adapting to the new country as well as changes in values and interactions between generations.

Acculturation Theory

Acculturation theory, as advanced by John Berry (1970, 1997, 2003), looks at the process of cultural (for example, customs, economic and political life) and psychological (for example, attitudes, identities, and social behaviors) change upon intercultural contact. Berry's (1990, 1997) model is based on the interaction between cultural maintenance (the extent to which individuals value and wish to maintain their cultural identity) and contact-participation (the extent to which individuals value and seek out contact with those outside their own group, and wish to participate in the daily life of the larger society). When immigrant families arrive in the United States, they are expected to adapt to their new host environment, learn a new language, and adopt the values, beliefs, and customs of the host culture. This adaption process begins as soon as immigrants and their families come in contact with the dominant culture and consists of the social and psychological interactions resulting from contact between individuals of different cultures (Berry, 1997; Ryder, Alden, and Paulhus, 2000).

Much of the increased attention paid to acculturation can be attributed to the post-1965 mass influx of immigrants from developing countries to the United States, when millions of immigrants started to originate mostly from ethnic minority groups (Bernstein, 2007). Although some scholars have charged that acculturation is negatively associated with cultural loss, that is, one culture's (the majority culture) overtaking the other culture (the minority culture), the concept is still used to explain the immigrant adaptation process.

Several different acculturation models have been proposed. The unidirectional or unilinear model of acculturation was an early theory proposed by Parks and Miller in the early twentieth century. According to these scholars, acculturation is unipolar in that the individual moves from a traditional lifestyle to one that is more assimilated. Specifically, the immigrant family starts adopting values and customs of the mainstream culture, leaving behind their own values and customs. The bidirectional model of acculturation (Berry, Trimble, and Olmedo, 1986) is more comprehensive and more widely accepted in the literature (see, for example, Cuellar, Arnold, and Maldonado, 1995). Berry's (1997) acculturation model focuses on two distinct axes, identification with home culture and identification with host culture, and is composed of four acculturation strategies (Berry, 1997): (1) integration/ bicultural (identification with both cultures), (2) assimilation/Americanized (identification with host culture), (3) separation/traditional (identification with home culture), and (4) alienation/marginalization (no identification). Integration refers to the process by which an immigrant identifies with and becomes involved with both cultures. Assimilation refers to the situation where an immigrant chooses to identify solely with the new culture. Separation refers to the instance when an immigrant is involved only in the traditional culture, and alienation/marginalization is characterized by the lack of involvement with and rejection of both cultures. These acculturation models offer insights into multifaceted interactions between immigrants and the dominant culture and help to explain more subtly the experiences of immigrant groups and allowing for an understanding of how individuals' cultural backgrounds play a role in adaptation (Berry and Sam, 1997).

Assimilation Theory

Assimilation refers to the process by which members of immigrant groups and host societies come to resemble one another (Alba and Nee, 2003). According to the classical assimilation theory of immigrant adaptation, immigrants tend to gradually lose their distinctive cultural traits and become assimilated into the dominant culture and social structure in the host country; distinctive ethnic traits such as native languages, cultural values, or ethnic enclaves are disadvantageous and negatively affect the assimilation process (Gordon, 1964).

Portes and Rumbaut (1996) argue that this linear view fails to explain the varied assimilation processes among and within immigrant groups, proposing three distinctive patterns of immigrant assimilation. The first is one of upward mobility, whereby the immigrant group economically advances quite rapidly and is integrated socially and politically into the middle class in a manner that is analogous to classical assimilation theory. For those groups, Americanization may lead to smooth adaptation and upward social mobility. The second pattern is acculturation and assimilation into the urban underclass, which leads to poverty and downward mobility. In this case, becoming Americanized may mean assimilating into the poor, underprivileged segment of society. The third pattern is selective acculturation, whereby immigrants retain certain cultural values and practices while engaging in selected mainstream practices of the host society (Portes and Rumbaut, 1996; Portes and Zhou, 1993; Zhou, 1997). While segmented assimilation theory has been helpful in highlighting the process by which first- and second-generation immigrants incorporated into American society, the theory itself is not without criticism (see Jung, 2009). Some scholars argue that the terms *assimilation, acculturation*, and *adaptation* implicitly refer to Americanization or cultural separation, grounded in the notion of similarity—"to assimilate is to become less different" (Jung, 2009, p. 381). In other words, this theory might separate minority immigrant culture from the mainstream American values in a way that suggests it is negative, inferior, or deficient (Jung, 2009; Oh and Cooc, 2011).

The concept of selective acculturation emphasizes that there is more than one way of "becoming American" and that succumbing to Americanization is not necessarily beneficial (Bankston and Zhou, 1997; Zhou, 1997). Selective acculturation describes adaptation in which ethnic cultural values and practices support participation in mainstream American society (Portes and Rumbaut, 2001). This cultural shift results in a bicultural existence and is supported by conditions such as a co-ethnic community, engagement in local institutions such as churches, restaurants, and schools, and a pace of cultural change that allows many elements of the home culture to be sustained (Portes and Rumbaut, 2001).

According to selective acculturation, retaining ethnic cultural values and practices can lead to upward mobility, allowing movement into the middle class of the host country. For example, Zhou and Bankston's (1996) study on Vietnamese youth reveals that intense participation in Vietnamese community activities (which are nonacculturative in the classical view) may actually facilitate assimilation into American society. Through strong Vietnamese community networks, Vietnamese students were encouraged to do well in the U.S. schools and participated successfully in that social institution, thereby increasing their economic mobility. Given the fundamental role cultural values play in the educational performance and social mobility of immigrants (Alba and Nee, 1997; Portes and Zhou, 1993), the process by which immigrant-origin students keep their cultural values intact while adjusting to educational systems is important to understanding educational outcomes. As another example, Mexican immigrants who retain the cultural values of their native country are less likely to be in conflict with their parents, remaining somewhat protected from the negative effects of assimilation (Portes and Zhou, 1993).

Context of Reception in Immigrant Assimilation

Portes and Rumbaut (2001) further expand on segmented assimilation theory by specifying the factors that influence disparate immigration adaptation processes and outcomes. They identify three relevant background factors that shape the experiences of immigrants: (1) individual characteristics, (2) family structure (for example, human capital or cultural traits), and (3) the larger social context the immigrant encounters in the new country. Portes and Zhou (1993) maintain that this last factor, described as the context of reception, plays an important role in immigrant assimilation patterns. This context of reception shapes how immigrants become involved in the host country's cultural, social, and economic practices. For example, research suggests that racial stereotypes might affect the assimilation paths of certain immigrant groups more than others (Portes and Rumbaut, 2001). Immigrants of color may assimilate less easily than White immigrants because of racial stereotypes and the negative reception of immigrants. Therefore, the communal reception of members of an ethnic group affects the quality of co-ethnic communities, and the extent to which they are present to support members as they arrive in the host country (Nuñez, 2004). Immigrants who can live in geographic proximity to a similar ethnic community have access to social and economic resources that aid in the ability to build a life in the new host country as well as to protect them from the stereotypes and prejudices of that country's society (Portes and Rumbaut, 2001).

Applicability of Segmented Theory to Student Persistence

While the process of immigration and assimilation is longer than the time it takes to enter and complete college, the foregoing theoretical insights may be useful in understanding the persistence experiences of immigrant college students. Classical assimilationists or social integrationists would contend that college students must fully adopt the norms of the college in order to succeed.

However, selective acculturation suggests that immigrant students from different backgrounds might not need to fully adopt the dominant cultural norms of a college in order to persist and succeed (Nuñez, 2004). Although a social integrationist perspective may assert that ethnic association can be detrimental to students' ability to persist because it may lead to campus balkanization (Antonio, 2001; D'Souza, 1991), the roles played by ethnic communities or subcultures can be crucial to providing necessary support and resources for immigrant students from disadvantaged backgrounds (Kim, 2009; Solórzano and Villalpando, 1998).

According to segmented assimilation theory, immigrant families and children retain certain cultural values and practices, while at the same time engaging in the values and practices of the mainstream host society (Portes and Rumbaut, 2001). As such, the concept of selective acculturation parallels immigrant college students' feelings of membership and participation in college life with respect to how students relate to past family and community experiences as they enter a new environment. This means the context of reception used in segmented assimilation theory can be applied in higher education as well (Keller and Tillman, 2008; Nuñez, 2004). For example, negative stereotypes and perceptions about immigrant students by the college community may influence their integration into and success in college (Montreuil and Bourhis, 2001; Rumbaut, 1994). Such negative stereotypes would influence these students' sense of belonging in the college campus (Hurtado and Carter, 1997).

Viewing immigrant students' experiences with selective acculturation in mind, persistence may be understood as a *selective adaptation* rather than full participation in the academic and social domains of the college. Unlike the integrationists' viewpoint that minority immigrant students are less likely to persist in college because they do not fully participate in the dominant culture of the college (Nuñez, 2004), it seems that immigrant students may be able to incorporate aspects of their less-mainstream identity into selected parts of the mainstream college culture. Therefore, selective adaptation in the college context may involve the student balancing and negotiating identity, immigrant cultural values, family, and community with the academic and social aspects of college life.

Social Capital Theory

In order to better understand immigrant students' college experiences and persistence, this section provides an overview of existing social capital theories drawing primarily on the work of Bourdieu, Coleman, and Lin. These theories prove useful in examining how immigrant students develop relationships with families, peers, university staff and faculty, and the external community, and which types of student relationships influence their adaptation to and persistence in college. Inspired by the work of sociologists Pierre Bourdieu and James Coleman, the theoretical export of social capital has been gaining attention from educational researchers and policy makers, who are attempting to determine its relationship to educational outcomes and improve the condition of education (Dika and Singh, 2002).

Bourdieu's Social and Cultural Capital[5]

Bourdieu (1986) defines social capital as "the aggregate of the actual or potential resources which are linked to possession of a durable network of more or less institutionalized relationship of mutual acquaintance or recognition" (p. 248). He argues that social capital consists of resources such as social networks that add to one's cultural capital and that the volume of social capital possessed depends on the size of the network of connections individuals can mobilize. Bourdieu's concept of social capital is composed of two elements: (1) the social relationship that allows individuals access to resources and (2) the amount and quality of those resources (Portes, 1998). This framework draws on the premise of social reproduction, primarily focusing on how membership in particular groups can create an advantage for some individuals. Essentially, Bourdieu views social capital as a mechanism the dominant social class uses to maintain and reproduce its social position (Lin, 1999a, 1999b). Bourdieu's social capital is inextricably linked to the concepts of cultural capital, habitus, and field.

Cultural capital is forms of acquired knowledge, skills, and inherited cultural competencies that provide signals to individuals as to how one behaves in order to adapt socially and gain a higher status (Bourdieu, 1986). This cultural capital exists in three distinct ways: (1) embodied (disposition of mind and body and acquired properties of one's self), (2) objectified (cultural goods), and (3) institutionalized (academic credentials or qualifications). In the embodied state, capital is strongly linked to one's *habitus*—a person's character, daily practices, perception of the environment, and way of thinking (Bourdieu, 1977). For example, linguistic capital, defined as the mastery of and relation to language, in the sense that it represents ways of speaking, can be understood as a form of embodied cultural capital (Bourdieu, 1990). In the objectified state, capital means things that are owned, such as scientific instruments or works of art. These cultural goods can be transmitted physically as an exercise in economic capital and symbolically as cultural capital. However, it is not simply the ownership of cultural goods but rather the ability to use and enjoy what one owns that matters (Tierney, 1999). The institutionalized state is the institutional recognition of the cultural capital held by an individual, often exemplified by academic credentials or qualifications suggesting an individual has acquired the capital (for example, college degree) necessary to assume a particular position in society. This allows easier conversion of cultural capital to economic capital by guaranteeing a certain monetary value for a certain institutional level of achievement (Bourdieu, 1990; Tierney, 1999).

Bourdieu argues that an individual's actions cannot be fully understood except in relation to the social context in which those actions occur (Bourdieu and Wacquant, 1992). His notion of *habitus* describes the ways in which individual actions and societal structures are linked (Bourdieu, 1977). Habitus is the internalized set of dispositions and preferences that subconsciously defines an individual's reasonable actions (Bourdieu and Wacquant, 1992; Horvat, 2001; McDonough, 1997). The individual agent develops habitus in response to determining structures such as class, family, and education and the external conditions (field) they encounter (Bourdieu, 1977). Thus, habitus reflects the internalization of structural boundaries and constraints and determines what is possible for an individual (Horvat, 2001).

Educational researchers have adopted the concept of cultural capital to illuminate how embedded the dominant middle-class norm is in families and the school climate (Horvat, 2001; Lareau, 2001; McDonough, 1997). For their purposes, Lamont and Lareau (1988) define cultural capital as "widely shared, high status cultural signals (attitudes, preferences, formal knowledge, behaviors, goods, and credentials) used for social and cultural exclusion" (p. 156). In other words, cultural capital is understood here as class-based socialization of culturally relevant skills, abilities, norms, and knowledge acquired primarily through family customs and education (Winkle-Wagner, 2010). Walpole (2007) notes the complexity of the term social class, indicating that understanding the role social class plays in influencing educational experiences and outcomes is critically important to improving the lives of economically and educationally challenged students, such as immigrant-origin students who are the first of their family members to attend college. Since prior research indicates that immigrant parents often hold a belief that their lives and those of their children after immigration into a new host country would be far better than in the country they left (Suárez-Orozco and Suárez-Orozoco, 2001), this notion of cultural capital asserts that, for example, Asian immigrant parents encourage their children to assimilate the norms, knowledge, and values of the White middle class (Ngo and Lee, 2007).

Cultural capital can be acquired not only from the status of the family but also from an institution such as college or university. Formal education clearly plays an important role in transmitting cultural values and reinforcing class privilege between generations (Bourdieu, 1986). For example, Lareau's (1987) qualitative work examines how social class influences the relationship between family and school and the ways in which low-socioeconomic- and high-socioeconomic-status parents utilize the social network to obtain information about schooling. She concludes that parents' information about and participation in their children's schooling experiences is closely related to social class (Lareau, 1987). Bourdieu (1977) argues that educational institutions reproduce social class by mimicking the uneven social and cultural resources of members of society. Parents are important sources of cultural capital, attitudes, and knowledge that make the educational system a comfortable, familiar place in which they can succeed easily, so children from wealthy families who maximize their advantage by investing their cultural capital are more likely to secure higher and durable academic profitability than those from working-class families (Bourdieu, 1986).

Bourdieu's concept of cultural capital is helpful to policymakers and educational researchers in understanding minority student persistence and success because it identifies the factors required to attain a college degree (see McDonough, 1997; McDonough, Ventresca, and Outcalt, 2000; Perna, 2000; Perna and Titus, 2005; Valadez, 1993; Wells, 2008). Immigrant-origin students need to acquire the cultural capital that majority students typically inherit. They need the requisite embodied capital to be able to interpret and decode different cultural objects, as well as objectified capital such as access to resources and the ability to perform. They also need institutionalized capital, such as a college degree. However, from Bourdieu's perspective, individuals are seen not as social agents struggling with cultures and creating conditions for change and empowerment but as mere actors who encapsulate their experiences and perceptions, leading to the reproduction of inequities (Tierney, 1999).

Coleman's Social Capital

The definition of social capital offered by Coleman (1988) is a closed system of social relations and networks between individuals and among groups. Focusing on the relational networks of family, community, and schools as a way to understand the impact of education on children, the concept of social capital produces value for persons or a group within a social organization. In turn, the value held by social capital identifies certain aspects of social structure and its function (Coleman, 1988). Coleman (1988) posits that social capital facilitates the transfer of human capital from parents to children. Children are strongly affected by their parents' human capital, a fact that stresses the role of social capital in communicating the norms, trust, and social controls that an individual must understand and adopt in order to succeed (see Portes and Sensenbrenner, 1993; Schneider, 2000).

Coleman (1988) examines how parental involvement can build social capital, suggesting that social capital is derived from two types of relationships: (1) the relationship between a child and his or her parents and (b) the relationships between a child's parents and other adults, particularly adults who are connected to the school that the child attends. He views the effort and resources that parents invest in the development of their children as critical to academic achievement (Coleman, 1988). Children who come from families with little human capital (for example, having limited formal education) are disadvantaged in the process of generating social capital. Coleman (1988), however, also argues that such human capital may be irrelevant to outcomes for children if parents are not an important part of their lives. In other words, if the human capital possessed by parents is not complemented by social capital embodied in family relations, it would not facilitate the child's educational growth regardless of the amount of human capital the parents possess (Coleman, 1988).

Although Bourdieu and Coleman agree that the value of social capital exists in relationships and ties between individuals who affect the access, acquisition, accumulation (Bourdieu, 1986) or transfer of human or cultural capital to others (Coleman, 1988), differing viewpoints are also evident between the two (Dika and Singh, 2002). Stemming from his theoretical scheme of social reproduction, Bourdieu views social capital as a means of reproduction of dominant social class, emphasizing structural constraints and unequal access to institutional resources based on race, gender, and class (Lareau, 2001). However, Coleman sees social capital as a positive social control, wherein a social relation is characterized by trust, norms, and information channels, meaning it is ultimately the family's responsibility to adopt certain norms and utilize information to increase a child's chance of success in education (Dika and Singh, 2002).

Lin's Social Networks

Drawing upon the work of Bourdieu and Coleman, Lin (2001) developed a theory of social capital to explain how the social network or the social structure constrains or enables access to resources embedded within the social structure. Social capital is defined in this case as "resources embedded in a social structure, which can be mobilized when an actor wishes to increase the likelihood of success in a purposive action" (Lin, 2001, p. 24). There are three elements fundamental to this version of social capital: (1) resources embedded within the network, (2) access to those resources through relationships, and (3) the use of the resources for purposive action. Lin (1999a, 1999b) proposes that access to and use of social resources can lead to better socioeconomic status. Further, he maintains that access to and use of social resources is in part determined by positions in the hierarchical structure and by the strength of ties (Lin, 2001).

Bourdieu and Coleman view closure and density of a group as a distinctive advantage of social capital. Bourdieu (1986) suggests that network density or closure is required for the dominant class to preserve its status and maintain resources. Similarly, Coleman (1988) asserts that network closure promotes effective communication and social norms as well as reinforces shared expectations, goals, and values through mutual recognition and acknowledgment. In contrast, Lin (2001) contends that network closure is not always required; although closed networks or strong ties may effectively preserve social status or resources, weak ties may conversely enable an individual to gain access to resources that would have otherwise been unavailable. Accordingly, weak ties may serve as a bridge to networks that possess information and resources different from those provided by strong ties or an individual's family and close friends. Lin (2001) argues that although individuals generally establish relationships with those who have a similar socioeconomic status and set of cultural values, some may seek relationships with those of higher status in order to access and acquire additional resources.

While each of these concepts of social capital is unique, there are common threads by which they are linked. Table 3 summarizes the assumptions behind each view of social capital, the domain in which empirical work might be guided by each assumption, level of analysis, and the operational focus.

Immigrants and Social Capital

In postsecondary education, immigrant students with limited human and cultural capital can benefit from the development of relationships with caring individuals and social connections with faculty, staff, and peers. For immigrant communities, the ability to draw on social capital may be particularly important (see Kao, 2004; Noguera, 2004; Portes, 1997; Portes and Sensenbrenner, 1993; Stepick, 1996; Zhou and Bankston, 1994; Zhou and Kim, 2006), especially given a possible deficit in cultural and human capital. The fact that some ethnic minority immigrant communities have very high educational success may be related to the extent and form of social capital available within their social networks (Stanton-Salazar, 2001, 2011; Stanton-Salazar and Dornbusch, 1995; Stanton-Salazar and Spina, 2003).

Research on immigrant social capital maintains that social ties are essential for economic survival and adaptation to a new society (see Damm, 2009; Liu,

TABLE 3
Foundational Perspectives of Social Capital Theories

	Bourdieu	Coleman	Lin
Underlying Assumption	Social capital for individual advancement and for reproduction of class	Family structures/social relationship enable exchanges of social capital for physical and/or human capital	Access and use of resources embedded in social networks
Level of Analysis	Individual or Group	Individual or group (family, school, and community)	Individual
Operational Focus	Exchange of values of social capital	Exchange values of social capital	Exchange of values of social capital
	Social capital vis-à-vis group factions within mainstream culture	Social capital manifested in trust norms, sanctions	Social capital manifest in strong and weak ties

Adapted from Lin (1999a, 1999b) and Ream (2001).

Ong, and Rosenstein, 1991; Massey, 1987; Menjívar, 2000; Portes and Rumbaut, 2001). Based on the strength of social ties, relatives, friends, and community members may offer immigrants housing, loans of money, and assistance in finding employment and orientation in the destination community (Massey, Alarcon, Durand, and Gonzalez, 1987). Immigrants rely heavily on kinship, friendship, neighborhood, community, or other ties, making social networks important in adaptation to a new environment (Massey, 1987; Menjívar, 2000; Portes, Haller, and Guarnizo, 2002; Zhou and Bankston, 1994). Social networks facilitate the building of human and cultural capital, thereby allowing upward social mobility and economic advancement (Bankston and Zhou 2002; Zhou and Bankston 2001).

Some studies have also indicated that in spite of their lack of attachment to outside networks, immigrant families draw on social capital stemming from familial or ethnic networks (see Portes, 1998; Zhou, 1997). Portes and MacLeod (1996) suggest that ethnic immigrant groups who were well received in the United States have been able to build stronger communities and networks to facilitate the development of social capital, with subsequent positive effects on their children's educational outcomes. Such well-received immigrant groups are found to have better academic outcomes regardless of socioeconomic status, suggesting that the internal character of the community plays a key role in encouraging immigrant students to achieve (Portes and MacLeod, 1996).

After examining the effects of social capital on immigrant students' academic achievement, Stanton-Salazar and Dornbusch (1995) concluded that Mexican high school students with higher grades and expectations generally had "greater social capital than their counterparts with lower grades and expectations" (p. 130); such students also have greater ties to institutional agents who could provide them with informational support. Similarly, White and Kaufman (1997) found that social capital is a significant predictor of high school completion among both immigrants and U.S.-born ethnic groups after controlling for factors such as grades, educational expectations, and familial socioeconomic status. They found that social capital "can buffer the risks associated with foreign birth and lower socioeconomic origins" (p. 397). However, Portes (2000) cautions against attributing effects solely to social capital, arguing that immigrant success, though initially appearing to be a result of positive effects of social capital, may in fact be attributable to other factors, such as the cultural capital that some individuals derive from ethnicity or the treatment of certain immigrant groups by broader society.

Although social capital seems promising as a theoretical construct in advancing our understanding of the educational experiences of immigrant students, most scholarly attention with respect to this concept has focused on college access. Enriquez (2011) sought to find ways in which social capital was accessed to successfully navigate K–12 institutions in pursuit of higher education, arguing that we need a more grounded understanding of how marginalized individuals develop and use social capital. Enriquez found that undocumented immigrant students receive emotional and financial support from multiple sources, including family members, peers, and teachers. However, undocumented students also need informational resources specific to their legal status, which tend to be provided by other undocumented students, rather than by traditional institutional agents. Using data from the National Education Longitudinal Study of 1988, Kim and Schneider (2005) examined the effects of social capital on different pathways to postsecondary education (two-year college, four-year college, or no postsecondary enrollment) among immigrant students. They refined the theory of social capital to take into account alignment between parents' and immigrant students' goals and actions. The study indicated that the effect of parents' education on students' selectivity in college choice depended on the alignment of parents and students regarding expectation and action. Despite a growing body of literature that examines the role of social capital in facilitating or inhibiting academic achievement and college access, little attention has been paid to examining social networks or social ties as strategies for immigrant student persistence in college. Drawing on the educational experiences of forty-nine ethnic minority immigrant students from a large public midwestern university, Kim's (2009) qualitative research found that minority immigrant students tended to rely on peer networks of the same ethnicity rather than institutional agents when seeking assistance in adapting to the college environment. Ethnic peer network membership on campus played a positive role in helping minority immigrant students adjust academically to college and persist from first to second year.

In higher education, immigrant students' different backgrounds may influence their abilities to persist. Structural characteristics of the college environment such as institutional agents including faculty, staff, and peers, can provide access to resources and support for these students. However, institutional structure may also limit the ability of immigrant students to develop trusting relationships with institutional agents. The interaction of immigrant students with key individuals inside and outside the college community may be viewed in terms of the student's integration with the overall student body as well as with an ethnic subculture or community. Strong ties with family, peers, staff, and faculty may help immigrant students adapt to the college environment and achieve success in college. Membership in ethnic communities or subcultures may also provide students with the opportunity to associate with others from similar backgrounds and may offer them needed academic, social, and emotional support resources. The availability of social capital does not always ensure persistence and success for the immigrant student. The values of the student's subculture and immigrant culture may not be entirely congruent with those of the larger dominant campus community, and immigrant students may feel less integrated with the larger campus community but well integrated into their own ethnic subcultures within the college campus. As Bourdieu and Passeron (1979) point out, despite having fewer resources on which to draw, immigrant students from disadvantaged backgrounds may succeed educationally through strong social ties with selected groups of individuals.

Conclusion

Immigrant-origin students are the fastest-growing segment of the U.S. population and will transform the educational and labor landscapes in the coming decades. These students encounter a unique set of challenges and often face forms of discrimination while adopting attitudes, beliefs, and behaviors that may conflict with those of their family, community, and homeland (Harklau, 1998). In order to evaluate any discrimination immigrant students encounter in higher education settings, neo-racism offers some valuable insight into barriers to college transition and college adjustment based on race and cultural or national identity. Although the social-ecological perspective in higher education research is just now emerging, it has already proven to be a useful framework, providing a look at broader contexts and co-occurring factors, as well as critical dimensions that shape diverse immigrant students' educational experiences that have been neglected in literature. We hope that scholars and researchers will pursue further research using a social-ecological framework to advance our understanding of immigrant students' educational experiences in higher education.

Immigrant students' college adaptation experiences have been of increasing interest to higher education researchers as their numbers continue to rise. The confluence of sociological, psychosocial, financial, and institutional influences on immigrant student persistence and their negotiation of collegiate experiences merits further examination. Few studies have systematically explored the experiences of immigrant college students. For these students, adaptation into the college environment is analogous to acculturating into a segment of American society. Although the notions of *acculturation, adaptation,* and *assimilation* have been used at times to imply that integrating into American society means adoption of the mainstream American culture and values, we argue that this phenomenon is a complex and dynamic process in which immigrant students are active agents in negotiating cultures and forming their own sense of identity while navigating cultural, sociopolitical, and geographic boundaries (Hoerder, Hebert, and Schmitt, 2006; Oh and Cooc, 2011). During these processes, social capital plays a critical role in negotiating and interpreting social relations for educational and career goals. In other words, we argue that issues related to a sense of belonging, adaptation, and inclusion/exclusion are influenced by social capital—the ability to take advantage of available resources in order to facilitate transitions to and persistence in college.

Access to Higher Education for Immigrant Students

THE RISING U.S. IMMIGRANT POPULATION has transformed the demographic profile of the nation in recent decades, and educating immigrant-origin students is now of the utmost national importance (Capps and others, 2005; Lee and Suarez, 2009). Immigrant access to higher education is affected by various factors, including race and ethnicity, cultural values, language and literacy level, socioeconomic status, country of origin, and length of residence in the United States. For example, immigrants from Latin America, especially those from Mexico and Central America, tend to enroll in U.S. postsecondary institutions at much lower rates than do their native-born counterparts and immigrants from other regions (Patten, 2012). Those who come to the United States between the ages of thirteen and nineteen years have the lowest levels of college attainment (Erisman and Looney, 2007). Students who arrive at even younger ages may still need to develop the English skills necessary for a successful academic performance while seeking higher education (Ruiz-de-Velasco and Fix, 2000).

While research has shown that immigrant students generally have high expectations for higher education, often higher than their native-born peers (Goyette and Xie, 1999; Hao and Bronstead-Bruns, 1998; Portes and Rumbaut, 2001; Rumbaut and Portes, 2001; Wells, 2010), on average, these expectations do not always match actual educational outcomes; immigrant students often experience lower postsecondary enrollment rates compared to their native-born counterparts. Over the past ten years, overall college enrollment rates have increased for the foreign-born population, but continue to lag behind the native-born. The gap in postsecondary enrollment rates among young adults between the ages of eighteen and twenty-four years has slightly widened between the foreign-born and native-born population (8.8 percent point difference in 2010 compared with 8.6 percent point difference in 2000) (Patten, 2012).

Given the great demand for advanced skills and training beyond high school in today's knowledge-intensive global economy, access to higher education has become increasingly important. In this chapter, we review some of the major factors that may positively or negatively affect immigrant students when transitioning to college. We examine areas commonly seen by existing literature as important in facilitating access to college among immigrant student groups, including (1) generational status, (2) socioeconomic status, (3) (limited) English language proficiency, (4) parental expectations and involvement, and (5) financial aid. It should be noted, however, that these are not the only determinants of college readiness and attendance. Rather, the confluence of these interrelated factors acts on immigrant-origin students as they enter into postsecondary education in complex ways.

Generational Status

Over the past decade, increasing attention has been paid to immigrant education in K–12 settings, resulting in an abundance of research on the factors and conditions that affect educational outcomes in secondary schools, such as geographic origin, race and ethnicity, age at immigration, generational status, and language minority status. Researchers generally agree that both first- and second-generation immigrants are at least as likely as to attend college, if not more likely, than their native-born counterparts of the same ethnicity. Some scholars argue that this advantage is derived from the fact that that most people who immigrate to the United States typically do so by choice and therefore arrive already motivated to succeed (see Bennett and Lutz, 2009; Kao, 2004). Immigrants also tend to possess the resources needed to relocate to a new country (Chiswick, 1999; Fukuyama, 1993). The optimist theory states that recent immigrants may have greater faith in the use of education to achieve upward mobility than their more established racial or ethnic minority peers in the later generations (Gibson and Ogbu, 1991). Immigrant students tend to have higher educational aspirations and stronger beliefs in the importance and usefulness of education than their native-born peers (Fuligni, Tseng, and Lam, 1999).

After considering both generational status and ethnicity, Hagy and Staniec's (2002) study suggested that immigrants' generational status influences their postsecondary enrollment decisions. Findings indicated that first- and second-generation Asian immigrants were significantly more likely to enroll in public institutions, both two- and four-year, while second-generation Hispanics and native Blacks tended to enroll in both public and private four-year institutions. Also, considering the effects of generational status (first, second, third, or later), Rong and Brown (2001) looked at years of schooling completed among Europeans, Africans, and Caribbean Blacks, and found a significant relationship between generation and years of schooling. Their research indicated that the educational attainment of the second-generation was significantly higher than that of first-generation and third-generation, particularly for Europeans and those from the Caribbean, though not for Africans.

The extant literature indicates that parental education levels are correlated with students' college aspirations and educational attainment, which also vary by generational status across racial/ethnic groups (Feliciano, 2006). In 2007–2008, among first-generation immigrant undergraduates enrolled in U.S. postsecondary institutions, 38 percent of Asians and 55 percent of Hispanics had parents who did not attend college, compared with 33 percent of all undergraduates (U.S. Department of Education, 2012b). However, only 28 percent of second-generation Asian undergraduates had parents who did not attend college, compared with 54 percent of second-generation Hispanic students, indicating differences in parents' postsecondary attendance by generational status across racial/ethnic groups.

Socioeconomic Status

Recent immigrants can be divided into two distinct social classes: educated professionals who enter the country to work in science, technology, engineering, and mathematics (STEM fields), and those who are poor and arrive in the United States as unskilled laborers seeking better opportunities for their families or a safe haven from political unrest in their home countries (Baum and Flores, 2011). While highly educated professional immigrants can provide their children with the resources needed to achieve academic success, such as better schools, assistance with assignments, and knowledge and advice on how to navigate the educational system (Suárez-Orozco and Suárez-Orozco, 2009), the latter group, composed of poor (working-class) immigrants, refugees, and undocumented immigrants struggle socioeconomically as well as academically (Baum and Flores, 2011; Lew, 2006; Louie, 2004).

An immigrant family's socioeconomic background, as measured by parental income, education, and occupation, has a powerful effect on that student's academic ability, educational outcomes, and occupation (Louie, 2005). Using data from the Current Population Survey (CPS), Borjas (2011) reveals that about one-third of the children of immigrants (including first- and second-generation immigrants) live in poverty—15 percent more than native children. This situation continues well into young adulthood, with consequences such as low academic achievement, higher school-dropout rates, and low postsecondary enrollment rates. Many immigrant students from low socioeconomic backgrounds attend overcrowded schools that are ill-equipped to meet their needs, staffed with inexperienced or disinterested teachers, and plagued by high dropout rates (Lopez, 2003; Ruiz-de-Velasco, Fix, and Clewell, 2001; Suárez-Orozco, Suárez-Orozco, and Todorova, 2008). For instance, more first-generation Asian (35 percent) and Hispanic (36 percent) undergraduates came from the low-income group, compared with 25 percent of all undergraduates in 2007–2008 (U.S. Department of Education, 2012b). Socioeconomic conditions differ among immigrants by country of origin. Though a similar percentage of the foreign-born and native-born population lived in poverty in 2010 (18.6 percent versus 14.8 percent, respectively), within the immigrant population, poverty rates differ by region of birth (Patten, 2012). For example, 27.9 percent of all immigrants from Mexico lived in poverty, followed by 22.2 percent of immigrants from the Middle East, 20.9 percent of Central American immigrants, 19.1 percent of Caribbean immigrants, and 12.7 percent of immigrants from

South and East Asia (Patten, 2012). More alarmingly, 47.1 percent of immigrants younger than eighteen years of age from the Middle East lived in poverty, followed by 46.1 percent of immigrants from Mexico, 31.7 percent of Caribbean immigrants, and 29.9 percent of Central American immigrants, much higher than that of native-born counterparts (Patten, 2012).

This is not to say that poor immigrants cannot succeed academically, but rather that the road to academic success and college access is often challenging. While some immigrants successfully navigate the U.S. educational system, many others, especially Latino immigrants who tend to come from low socioeconomic backgrounds, drop out of high school, fail to gain access into U.S. colleges and universities, or once gaining access are unable to persist (Gándara and Contreras, 2009). For example, twelfth-grader Latinos average an eighth-grade reading level (Fry, 2003; Gándara and Contreras, 2009). As a result, Latinos have the highest high school dropout rates (48 percent) and the lowest college access and attainment rates of all racial/ethnic groups in the United States (Chapman, Laird, and KewalRamani, 2010; Perez Huber and others, 2006). Rumbaut (2005), however, has found variations in attainment rates within Latino and Asian immigrant communities. Using the Children of Immigrants Longitudinal Study (CILS), he examined the educational attainment rates of immigrant children in their mid-twenties who arrived in the United States before the age of eighteen years, whose parents came from Asian and Latin American countries. He found that while Chinese, Indians, and Koreans were the most educated subgroups, Mexicans, other Latinos, Cambodians, and Laotians had high dropout rates.

Researchers posit that low achievement rates among immigrant subgroups correlate with country of origin and immigrant status (Batalova and Fix, 2011). Batalova and Fix found that Chinese and Indian immigrants tend to come from wealthier families with higher educational attainment rates, as opposed to Laotian and Cambodian refugees, who have poorer educational attainment rates and less wealth. In another study, Solorzano, Villalpando, and Oseguera (2005) reported that 52 percent of Latinos graduated from high school, but when the students' country of origin was factored in, Cubans, Dominicans, and Puerto Ricans showed higher graduation rates than Mexicans and Salvadorians.

English Language Proficiency

The diverse ethnic immigrant population of the United States has caused the linguistic landscape of the country to change drastically in recent decades. U.S. Census data from 2000 indicates more than 460 languages were spoken by children at school nationwide (Garcia, Kleifgen, and Falchi, 2008; Kindler, 2002). The top ten languages spoken by immigrants aged five years and older were Spanish (35.5 million), Chinese (2.6 million), Tagalog (1.5 million), French Patois and Cajun (1.3 million), Vietnamese (1.2 million), German (1.1 million), Korean (1.0 million), Russian (900,000), Arabic (845,000), and African languages (780,000) (U.S. Census Bureau, 2009).

In 2010, more than half of the foreign-born population age five and older self-reported as limited English proficient (Patten, 2012). Most students with low English proficiency are born and raised in the United States, have at least one U.S.-born parent, and live in linguistically isolated families or attend linguistically isolated/segregated schools (Capps and others, 2005). In 2007, approximately 29 percent of African immigrants reported speaking English "not well" (Terrazas, 2009), while in 2009, 46.6 percent of Asians classified themselves as having limited English proficiency (LEP)[6] (Batalova, 2011). As is the case with LEP African immigrants, rates of limited English proficiency vary substantially by the individual's origin (Batalova, 2011; Terrazas, 2009). Among Hispanics, approximately 2.2 million immigrants self-reported as LEP (Skinner and others, 2010). Among first-generation immigrants who came to the United States at age sixteen or older, 80 percent of Hispanics were LEP, compared with 34 percent of non-Hispanic immigrants; among those who arrived in the United States before the age of sixteen years, 49 percent of Hispanics and 18 percent of non-Hispanic immigrants were LEP (Batalova and Fix, 2011).

According to the 2008 National Postsecondary Student Aid Study, 12 percent of undergraduate students in the United States come from a language minority (LM) background, reporting not having spoken English as the primary language in their home (U.S. Department of Education, 2012b). These linguistic minority students are primarily immigrant-origin, either first- or second-generation. Among first-generation immigrant undergraduates, almost three-quarters of Asians and more than 80 percent of Hispanics reported not speaking English as the first language in their home, compared with 41 percent of second-generation Asians and 52 percent of second-generation Hispanics (U.S. Department of Education, 2012b). However, few studies have explored rates of postsecondary enrollment and college attainment among immigrant students with linguistic minority backgrounds (Nuñez and Sparks, 2012; Rodriguez and Cruz, 2009). Klein, Bugarin, Beltranena, and McArthur (2004) found that among the traditional college-age cohort (eighteen to twenty-four years of age), students with linguistic minority status were less likely than others to enroll in college (28 percent versus 37 percent, respectively). In the 2004 Beginning Postsecondary Students Study, Nuñez and Sparks (2012) also found that students with linguistic minority backgrounds were far less likely than their nonlinguistic minority peers to enroll in selective institutions (13 percent versus 56 percent, respectively), again indicating the effect of linguistic minority status on postsecondary enrollment patterns.

Whether an LEP immigrant learns English depends on a variety of factors, including immediate surroundings. Waldorf, Beckhusen, Florax, and de Graaff (2010) analyzed the role of human capital in English language acquisition among Mexican and Asian immigrants residing in urban areas using data from the 2000 U.S. Census. Immigrants who lived in metropolitan areas among large communities of their own ethnic groups or subgroups were, on average, less likely to learn English than immigrants who lived in cities with small or no immigrant communities. Residing or working within an ethnic group allowed LEP immigrants to fulfill daily functions without learning English.

For this reason, it is important for educational institutions to provide LEP students with programs that allow them to develop English skills. Among those studied by Waldorf and her colleagues, 40 percent of Chinese and Mexican immigrants who had graduated from high school self-identified as proficient in English, compared with 23 percent of Chinese and Mexican immigrants who had not completed a high school education. They also found that 70 percent of college-educated Chinese and Mexican immigrants were fluent in English.

While it is clear that English language skills and development are positively associated with immigrant students' academic achievement and college preparation, many school districts fail to prepare LEP students for college. Many schools tend to place English language learners in low-track curriculums with limited exposure, if any, to core curriculum classes and electives designed to prepare students for college (Faltis and Coulter, 2008). Immigrant students with LEP are more likely than the general student population to underperform on standardized tests and to drop out of school (Gándara, 2007). Part of the problem facing LEP immigrant students is that they often face limited access to academic content, weak language instruction, and linguistic isolation (see Callahan, 2005; Harklau, 1994; Valdés, 2001). Nationwide, almost half of LEP students attend schools in high-poverty neighborhoods where 30 percent or more of students are LEP (Garcia, 2000; Ruiz-de-Velasco and Fix, 2000).

Acquiring language proficiency encompasses many components, including grammatical competence, communicative competence, and a change in attitudes toward one's own or another culture. While English language proficiency is the key to academic preparation for LEP immigrants, the delivery of actual content is also important to improving English language skills and academic literacy. For example, as reported by Russakoff (2011), teaching content in the student's native language, along with English language instruction, will significantly enhance reading and math skills. The majority of ESL programs, however, provide little or no native language instruction. Callahan (2005) examined data collected from 355 English language learners, of which 98 percent were Spanish speakers at one school in California. She found that academic preparation (instruction in math, science, and reading), rather than the acquisition of English proficiency, was the strongest predictor of academic success.

Focusing solely on language acquisition proves detrimental to the educational success of foreign-language speakers. Callahan, Wilkinson, Muller, and Frisco (2009) studied the academic effects of English as a second language (ESL) placement on English language learners, and found that schools continued to prioritize English language acquisition at the expense of academic preparation. The misguided belief that students cannot learn with the rest of their classmates until they are fully proficient in English has left ESL students unable to acquire the academics needed to meet college entrance requirements (Callahan, 2005). Callahan posits that the most successful ESL programs expose students to academic content as they acquire English proficiency, since lower-level ESL track courses can only lead to higher high school dropout rates (Lopez, 2003).

In an effort to identify practices that would prepare English language learners for college, Bitter and Golden (2010) conducted a study in five schools in San Diego, California. Ten Spanish-speaking students, two teachers, and the principal were interviewed on the practices in place at the schools, which all touted academic preparation as a core goal. These practices included, but were not limited to, analytical writing, heterogeneous grouping, dual programs with a college, role models, tutoring, internships, well-trained and experienced ESL teachers, parent outreach, and college trips. Staff, parents, and students all deemed these practices successful. Acknowledging that there is no single model that can meet the particular needs of each diverse immigrant student population, it is important that ESL programs should have targeted professional development for teachers and literacy development instruction (American Youth Policy Forum, 2009, 2010; Short and Boyson, 2012).

Parental Involvement and Expectations

The decision to attend college is a complex process involving not only students who prepare for, apply to, and choose a school, but also parents, families, communities, and school personnel. Examining factors associated with students' college goals and enrollment choices reveals that parental involvement is positively related to children's college aspirations and academic preparation (Cabrera and La Nasa, 2000; Hossler, Schmit, and Vesper, 1999; Perna, 2000; Perna and Titus, 2005; Rowan-Kenyon, Bell, and Perna, 2008).

Student aspirations and parental expectations are vital to immigrant student access to higher education and have a direct relationship to academic performance (Fuligni and Witkow, 2004; Kao and Tienda, 1998; Zhou and Bankston, 1998). In general, research indicates that immigrant students have higher educational expectations than their native-born peers due to their parents' positive attitudes and optimism about immigrating to the United States in search of a better life (see Louie, 2001, 2004; Schneider and Lee, 1990). Studies that take into account racial/ethnic factors show that immigrants' aspirations and expectations help to drive educational attainment. Suárez-Orozco and Suárez-Orozco (1995) examined immigration and family life among Latino youth in the U.S. and found that determination to succeed was based on the understanding of sacrifices made by family so that the children could lead a better life. Their feelings of guilt "gave way to a determination to seize upon an opportunity" (Suárez-Orozco and Suárez-Orozco, 1995, p. 79). Moral capital, a type of aspirational capital, is foundational to a Latino child's educational success. In her ethnographic case study examining the role of low socioeconomic Latino parents in their children's' levels of college access, Auerbach (2006) found that moral capital, or messages concerning the importance of school, conveyed the value of education in career and social mobility. Constant reminders of the importance of studying and the need to do well in class in order to go to college were believed by parents to make a difference in their children's educational outcomes. These messages, or *consejos*, provided students with the confidence to persist. Encouragement, expectations for a better life, and an awareness of the sacrifice made by their parents helped children to achieve their educational goals (see also Orózco, 2008).

Parental expectations and involvement differ across immigrant groups (Mau, 1995, 1997). Mau (1997) conducted a quantitative study that examined parental influence on the academic achievement of Asian immigrants, Asian Americans, and Whites. Findings indicated that Asian academic success is associated with high expectations and the belief that deficiencies can be overcome with hard work. Parental involvement was not a predictor of Asian and Asian-American educational achievement, though; in contrast, it was a predictor for White Americans.

Financial, psychological, and structural barriers often limit working-class or low-income parents' involvement in their children's decisions (Hoover-Dempsey and Sandler, 1997; Louie, 2001; Perna, 2004). Louie's (2001) study, for example, points to marked differences between middle- and working-class Chinese immigrant parents in decisions related to the allocation of educational resources to facilitate opportunities to attend college and promote social mobility. Working-class Chinese immigrant parents relied on school resources or ethnic networks to obtain information about college to help their children to navigate the college transition while middle-class parents had their own knowledge about college and additional resources on which they draw. In her study of Chinese students from different socioeconomic backgrounds, Louie (2004) discussed the family as the reason Chinese students, regardless of their socioeconomic status, performed well academically. Both 1.5 and second-generation Chinese students took their parents' sacrifices and high expectations seriously, viewing them as helpful in attending college and moving up the socioeconomic ladder.

Kim and Kamnoetsin (2011) examined how immigrant parents' expectations and involvement shaped Chinese and Korean students' college decisions and how these students negotiated their parents' expectations. Findings suggested that although both Chinese and Korean immigrant parents held high academic expectations for their children, the level of parental involvement and the strategies for seeking educational resources adopted by these parents differ by social class and ethnicity. Immigrant parents from working-class backgrounds (no college education and labor-intensive jobs) adopted the strategies to utilize the resources available within their ethnic community. While both Korean and Chinese parents emphasized the value of education, the degree to which they actualized its value depended on their social position and financial resources. Overall, parents' involvement and expectations were instrumental for students in choosing a college and an academic major.

Financial Aid

The affordability of higher education remains a critical issue for many, but particularly for low-income students and families from immigrant backgrounds. For many students, it is becoming more difficult to pay for higher education because of the gap between increasing tuition prices and financial assistance. Fortunately for some low- and middle-income students, there are several programs that allow them (because of their household's low to moderate earnings) to access and pay for college. While naturalized citizens and legal permanent residents are typically eligible for in-state tuition in public higher education, similar to their native-born counterparts, considerable state-by-state and institution-by-institution variations exist for undocumented immigrant students, and those awaiting action on their applications for asylum and adjustment status, who are considered to be ineligible for federal aid and most forms of state aid (Gonzales, 2009; Gray, Rolph, and Melamid, 1996).

A primary reason such a large percentage of immigrants have a low socioeconomic status may be due to low rates of educational attainment (Lopez, 2006). Since financial aid has been found to positively influence access and persistence (Biswas, 2005), the federal and state government, as well as postsecondary institutions, need to reassess the financial aid currently available to the large and growing immigrant population. Data from the 2003–2004 National Postsecondary Student Aid Study indicates (foreign-born) immigrant students were more likely than undergraduate students to have higher unmet financial needs. Immigrant undergraduate students who depended on their parents for financial support were 86 percent more likely to come from the lowest-income quintile than other dependent undergraduate students, and 71 percent of dependent legal permanent residents were in the two lowest income quintiles (U.S. Department of Education, 2004).

Going to college is a process that involves navigating the complex financial aid system (Erisman and Looney, 2007). Access to financial aid is critical for many immigrant students who tend to be low-income, first-generation college attendees or LEP. In the past decade, the cost of a college education has risen far faster than inflation or family income. Exacerbated by the recent recessions, sharp declines in state revenues, and reduced federal funding for higher education, the rising cost of college has shifted the burden of paying for college from taxpayers to students and their families (Long and Riley, 2007). Moreover, recent heated debates on immigrant tuition bills have put undocumented immigrant students in danger of losing access to higher education.

A lack of knowledge of financial aid resources and how to access the various forms of financial aid has caused 850,000 financial aid–eligible students to neglect to file the Free Application for Federal Student Aid (FAFSA) (Avery and Kane, 2004; De La Rosa, 2006; King, 2004). Resident status (whether students are permanent residents or undocumented immigrants) also affects accessibility to financial aid resources. We provide a detailed discussion of federal and state policy on undocumented students, and how it affects their access to and financing of college, in the chapter on "undocumented students and higher education." Most immigrant students and parents from low socio-economic backgrounds learn about financial aid programs too late. Zarate and Pachon (2006) looked, at least in part, at what Latino immigrant students in California understood about financial aid. They found that the majority of students indicated financial aid was an important factor in the decision to attend college, but admitted that they were either not familiar with the various sources/types of available financial aid or believed that the aid available was designated for U.S. citizens only. Similarly, a survey conducted for the Sallie Mae Fund concluded that low-income Latino students received financial aid information later than higher-income Latino families, and that low-income families are not aware of many scholarships and grants (Sallie Mae Fund, 2003).

Almost 80 percent of high school students receive their information on financial aid as juniors or seniors from their high school coaches, counselors, or teachers (De La Rosa, 2006). This is especially true for low-SES Latino immigrants (Zarate and Pachon, 2006), who are 72 percent more likely to rely on counselors for financial aid information, compared with 34 percent of high-income students (Terenzini, Cabrera, and Bernal, 2001). Unfortunately, immigrant students do not have equal access to counseling (Lee and Ekstrom, 1987), and counselor bias may negatively impact college access. McDonough and Calderone (2004) examined what counselors knew about financial aid, how they disseminated information, and how they perceived the financial concerns of low-income immigrant students. Counselors frequently viewed these students as passive and afraid to apply to four-year colleges because of the cost. Instead of providing students with financial information that would alleviate their fears and encourage them to apply to more prestigious institutions, these counselors often steered students toward community college.

Other sources of financial aid information for high school students are available on the Internet, such as the FAFSA website, state financial aid websites, and college websites. The Internet now allows low-income immigrant students to easily search for information on financial aid. Vargas (2004) discussed the shift toward web-based information, examining whether or not this shift would exclude low-income immigrant students who do not own computers. He concluded that online sources can address the issues among underserved and underrepresented students associated with obtaining accurate financial aid information and college tuition. Later, Venegas (2006) investigated the impact of digital technology on low-SES immigrant urban high school students. While these students have access to computers in various settings, she found that college-bound Hispanic immigrant students faced technical difficulties in accessing information from web-based sources or were ambivalent about providing personal information on websites that were not affiliated with a college.

Conclusion

Greater access to college for immigrants is vital not only to the economic health of the country at large but also for the personal and economic well-being of immigrants and their families. Many issues need to be addressed in order to promote college access and enrollment for immigrant students and achieve a well-educated U.S. workforce. Academic preparedness may be accomplished through well-trained teachers, adequate resources, culturally sensitive curricula that build upon the strengths of the immigrant students, tutoring sessions, and outreach to parents and communities. Research has shown that immigrants generally value higher education and hold high academic expectations and college aspirations, but we must acknowledge that access to college differs across racial and ethnic groups, generations, and socioeconomic levels. Finally, knowledge about financial aid appears to be a key predictor in determining the likelihood of college attendance among various immigrant racial and ethnic groups. The lack of financial aid and an understanding of how to obtain it prevents thousands of immigrant students from accessing higher education, revealing a direct relationship between awareness of financial aid and college attendance. The federal and state government and all higher education institutions must once again direct the majority of available aid to low-income immigrant students who are closed out of a college education due to lack of finances.

Collegiate Experience of Immigrant Students

LARGE-SCALE RESEARCH HAS REVEALED THAT the number of immigrant students who complete a college degree is equal to or greater than that of their native counterparts (Betts and Lofstrom, 1998; Chiswick and DebBurman, 2004; Erisman and Looney, 2007; Fuligni and Witkow, 2004; Hagy and Staniec, 2002; Kao and Thompson, 2003; Ruiz-de-Velasco and Fix, 2000; Vernez and Abrahamse, 1996). However, these studies overlook important disparities in educational outcomes across immigrant subgroups. Scant research exists on which immigrant student groups actually transition to college, what educational experiences they have after matriculation, the challenges they face while in college, and to what extent postsecondary education outcomes (intellectual and interpersonal competence, identity development, career development, and postbaccalaureate outcomes) differ across various immigrant student groups. If immigrant students do fare as well in higher education as their native-born counterparts, scholarly attention might be well directed toward issues related to native-generation or other non-immigrant student populations. Existing studies do not, however, adequately address the quality and nuances of immigrant students' educational experiences while they are in college; specifically, they fail to describe how these students' collegiate attitudes, beliefs, and behaviors are shaped; they fall short of addressing the challenges that confront immigrant college students as they navigate the college environment; and they leave questions unanswered as to the ability of these students to negotiate their racial and ethnic identities. In order to build on the strengths and limitations in educational research on immigrant college students, our primary objective in this chapter is to critically review findings from empirical research across disciplines that address educational experiences of diverse immigrant student groups. In this chapter, we organize our synthesis into four broad categories: (1) college adjustment and persistence, (2) psychological development and acculturation, (3) social identity development, and (4) career aspirations and development (see Appendix for a summary of studies related to these four overarching research themes). Discussion and analysis of a particular subgroup of immigrant students, undocumented immigrants, will be provided in detail in the next chapter.

College Adjustment and Persistence

The transition to college is a critical period marked by a host of complex psychological, academic, social, and cultural challenges (Chickering and Reisser, 1993). Immigrant students may encounter pressure to adopt collegiate attitudes, beliefs, and behaviors that possibly conflict with those of family, community, and homeland (Harklau, 1998). Familial obligations may also act as a double-edged sword in college adjustment, as immigrant students can feel a sense of duty to contribute financially to the family along with great pressure to succeed academically (Fuligni and Pedersen, 2002; Kim, 2009). Other challenges include handling educational demands, meeting institutional expectations; motivating themselves to persist in college; completing academic requirements; and how satisfied they are with their academic work and college environment. How well a student grapples with these challenges is an important factor in student persistence. Using semistructured interviews with 82 Filipina college students from immigrant families (the majority of participants were first- and second-generation) at a large research university in Southern California, Maramba (2008) identified three primary themes in college adaptation experiences: (1) family/parent influence, (2) home obligations/gender differences, and (3) the importance of negotiating identity within both home and college experiences. Her study found that Filipina students felt pressure to do well academically in college while maintaining their duties at home. Relationships with parents and siblings also influenced the daily lives of these students on campus. This study suggests that student affairs practitioners might help students with an immigrant background by developing partnerships with their families to provide the necessary support for academic and personal success. In a study by Kim (2009), the analysis of interviews of forty-nine (1.5 generation) minority immigrant students at a large public institution in the Midwest, revealed that academics were at the center of college persistence, regardless of race, ethnicity, immigrant status, or socioeconomic background. Relationships with parents, siblings, and peers—in particular, peers from campus social networks and ethnic subcultures—played a critical role in the ability of these immigrant students to navigate the academic world.

Sy and Romero (2008) looked at how family responsibilities affected college retention of Latinas. Conducting semistructured interviews with twenty first- and second-generation Latinas, the researchers identified three key themes: (1) participants emphasized the need to be self-reliant to avoid placing a burden on their family; (2) the women did not feel obligated to financially support their families, but rather that their financial contributions were voluntary; and (3) they often felt responsible for taking a parenting role with their younger siblings. More effort is clearly needed to help Latina college students reduce their family obligations and maintain close relationships with family to facilitate adjustment to college.

Many researchers critique the concept of cultural integration, characterizing it as not adequate for an understanding of college persistence in minority students; instead, they argue for using the concept of "membership" or a "sense of belonging" (see Hurtado and Carter, 1997; Rendón, Jalomo, and Nora, 2000). Hurtado and Carter (1997) point to the importance of examining an individual's sense of connectedness with the campus community. Drawing on the Student Experience in the Research University (SERU) survey, a study based on responses from 55,433 undergraduate students at six large research institutions across the United States, Stebleton, Huseman, and Kuzhabekova (2010) found that immigrant college students (both first- and second-generation) consistently reported lower levels of sense of belonging and satisfaction compared to their native peers. Other studies have shown that when faculty and institutional staff (for example, advisors and counselors) provide a welcoming and nurturing learning environment for immigrant students and are cognizant of individual backgrounds and cultural differences, student adjustment to the college environment is less stressful (see Rocha-Tracy, 2009).

Considerable scholarly effort has been put into identifying factors associated with immigrant students' college persistence and degree completion at two-year and four-year institutions: family support and obligation, financial aid, cultural values that promote education, and precollege experience (see Bailey and Weininger, 2002; Conway, 2009, 2010; Erisman and Looney, 2007; Fuligni and Witkow, 2004; Zajacova, Lynch, and Espenshade, 2005). In general, immigrant students who come from low-income families or whose parents have no college experience are less likely to complete a college education.

Erisman and Looney (2007) found that undergraduate (foreign-born) immigrant students have higher-than-average unmet financial needs. More specifically, students in this category who depended on their parents for financial support were 86 percent more likely to come from the lowest-income quintile than other dependent undergraduate students, and 71 percent of dependent legal permanent residents were in the two lowest income quintiles. A growing body of evidence suggests that financial aid plays a significant role in degree completion for immigrant students, especially those from disadvantaged backgrounds, in conjunction with level of academic preparation, family responsibility, family income, and parental education (Baum and Flores, 2011; Erisman and Looney, 2007).

Fuligni and Witkow (2004) examined the postsecondary educational progress of youth from immigrant families, with results indicating that these students were likely to have the same level of postsecondary educational progress as their counterparts with American-born families. Approximately 650 youths from a range of ethnic and generational backgrounds participated in this longitudinal study in New York, San Francisco, and Los Angeles. Immigrant participants demonstrated the same levels of four-year institution enrollment, persistence, and degree completion as peers from American-born families. However, youth from immigrant families were more likely to support their families financially and to live with parents than those from American-born families. Variability among immigrant families suggested that children from families with higher incomes, higher levels of parental education, and from East Asian backgrounds were more likely to enroll and persist in postsecondary education.

Existing research has demonstrated that immigrant-origin students are more likely to persist in college, continuing education until a degree is completed. These studies provide some understanding of immigrant students' overall academic success levels once they enroll in colleges and universities. However, research has yet to explore the extent to which other factors contribute to college persistence in immigrants across diverse immigrant subgroups at different institutional settings. The bulk of current data on immigrant college students' educational outcomes, often measured by degree completion, has been quantitatively oriented, identifying factors or predictors that contribute to college success. What is lost is a nuanced understanding of and appreciation for process (how these factors result in positive outcomes), and the specific relationships between and among various factors. Immigrant students undergo a complex transformation as they come to understand the importance of learning and adapting to a new college environment while making sense of and finding ways to reconcile tensions and conflict arising from an ongoing negotiation of multiple roles and identities. Thus, it is important for future research to focus not only on identifying the characteristics of immigrant students who are likely to succeed in college, but also on identifying processes and factors that lead to college success.

Psychological Development and Acculturation

Acculturation is an important concept used to explore immigrants' psychological well-being, family conflict, and issues related to mental health (see Desai, 2006; Huang, 2006). Acculturation refers to contact between individuals or groups from different cultural backgrounds and the adaptation that takes place as a result of such contact (Berry, 1980, 1997). For many immigrant-origin students, acculturation is an important issue. Current research suggests that acculturation is multidimensional, consisting of behavioral (cultural practices such as language use and media preferences), affective (cultural identification such as a sense of membership with one's country of origin or host country), and cognitive (cultural values such as prioritizing one's own needs over one's family's needs) domains (Chirkov, 2009; Kim and Abreu, 2001; Rudmin, 2009; Schwartz, Unger, Zamboanga, and Szapocznik, 2010). Influenced primarily by psychological theory, some studies have examined how the development of self-esteem and mental health in immigrant students relates to college adaptation (see Huang, 2006; Hudson, Towey, and Shinar, 2008). Quantitative methodology, particularly psychometric instruments, has predominated in this line of research. In a study designed to measure acculturative stress in immigrant Chinese students, Chau (2006) quantitatively examined the relationship between acculturative stress and spirituality among sixty-three Chinese immigrant college students. Participants received a self-administered questionnaire developed to measure their levels of acculturative stress and spiritual well-being, with results indicating a significant correlation between the two. Respondents who had a higher level of spiritual well-being reported lower levels of acculturative stress, suggesting that spirituality and religious involvement could be used to cope with stress among Chinese immigrant college students. In another study, Huang (2006) investigated the relationship between acculturation, Asian cultural values, family conflict, and perceived stress in female Chinese immigrant college students. The sample consisted of sixty-six female Chinese immigrant college students between the ages of eighteen and thirty. All participants had resided in the United States for at least three years and immigrated to the United States from China or other Asian countries. Participants were given five self-administered questionnaires to complete: the Demographic Questionnaire, the Suinn-Lew Asian Self-Identity Acculturation Scale (SL-ASIA), Asian Values Scale (AVS), Asian American Family Conflict Scale (AAFCS), and Perceived Stress Scale-14 (PSS-14). Findings suggested that level of acculturation was negatively correlated with level of perceived stress, and level of adherence to Asian cultural values was positively correlated with level of perceived stress, establishing the possibility of a direct relationship between adhering to cultural values and higher perceived stress levels.

College students are often considered to be in the highest-risk category in terms of health risk behaviors. Among first- and second-generation immigrant students, extant research suggests that acculturation may be linked with many of the health risk behaviors common on college campuses, such as drug and alcohol use (Allen and others, 2008; Zamboanga, Raffaelli, and Horton, 2006). Addressing the effects of acculturation on health outcomes across race/ethnicity and within racial/ethnic groups, Schwartz and others (2011) examined the relationship between acculturation and health risk behaviors among 3,251 first- and second-generation immigrant students from thirty U.S. colleges and universities. Results indicated that both first- and second-generation immigrant students engaged in health risk behaviors at similar rates, but there were racial and ethnic differences in the link between acculturation and health risk behaviors. Among East Asian participants, the adoption of U.S. cultural practices and identification was positively associated with sexual risk taking and hazardous alcohol use; in comparison, among Black participants, heritage (native) cultural orientation was negatively correlated with alcohol use. For Hispanic participants, heritage-cultural practices were negatively associated with sexual risk taking, but ethnic identity was positively associated with these behaviors. This study suggests that immigrant-origin students who are more acculturated are more likely to take risks as compared with their less acculturated counterparts, yielding important implications for working with college students from immigrant families; retaining heritage cultural practices and values is important in reducing health-related risk behaviors.

A quantitative study by Buddington (2002) examined the relationship between level of acculturation and level of self-esteem among Jamaican immigrant college students ($n = 150$). Recently immigrated Jamaican students were not highly acculturated, indicating a positive correlation between the length of residency and the level of acculturation. Students' acculturation was not related to their level of self-esteem or state of depression, and those who were married to Jamaicans, who returned home to see their relatives and continued to communicate with them, had high academic achievement. The frequency of returning home was found to be inversely related to acculturation.

In sum, a growing body of literature has emerged pointing to a variety of factors that affect immigrant college students' psychological well-being: various economic, socio-psychological characteristics of the student and his/her community, as well as a series of historically determined contextual variables (Gibson, 1997; Neisser, 1986; Trueba, 1988). Parental and student beliefs, attitudes, goals, and routines, along with relationships with family, siblings, and peers, and development of spirituality seem to interact in determining the extent to which immigrant students cope with acculturative stress in college. Students' cultural origin and history, and socio-educational context also appear to be critical factors that, together with family background and individual characteristics, are linked to individual and group differences in psychological adjustment and the process of acculturation.

Social Identity Development

Despite a plethora of student development theories providing ways to understand students' intellectual, personal, and social growth (Pope, 2000), such as psychosocial, cognitive-structural, typology, person-environment, and social identity (Evans and others, 2010; McEwen, 2003), there is a dearth of research on incorporating social identities (race, ethnicity, gender, sexual orientation) into student development research and practices for the immigrant student population. Social identity development continues through early adulthood and is shaped and reshaped as individuals experience unfamiliar situations and assume new roles and responsibilities. In particular, the college years are a time when racial and ethnic identity development becomes increasingly critical to the success of a college student and the overall quality of his or her collegiate experiences. This is a time when students' sense of who they are and who they want to become is influenced by relationships with others in social surroundings (see Benesch, 2008; Brettell and Nibbs, 2009; Lee and Andrea, 2010; Louie, 2004). Consequently, the development of racial and ethnic identity in both students of color (Blacks, Asian Americans, and Latino Americans) and Whites has drawn increasing attention in college student developmental literature (Evans and others, 2010). Racial and ethnic identity development is integral to students' overall development and their educational experiences in college, particularly for immigrant students (Rumbaut, 1994). Immigrant students are often expected to simultaneously retain the language, values, and customs of their country of origin while acquiring those of the United States. They are also expected to interact with peers and institutional agents from both their own ethnic group and other cultures (Phinney, 1992; Phinney, Romero, Nava, and Huang, 2001; Smith, 1991).

The term *racial identity* refers to the process by which individuals define themselves based on racial categories in social contexts (Pizarro and Vera, 2001). Ethnic identity refers to aspects of one's self-concept derived from awareness and knowledge of membership in an ethnic group (Phinney, 1990; Sellers and others, 1997). The central role ethnicity plays in one's identity leads to the acquisition of certain values and beliefs, and engagement in behaviors consistent with the traditions and heritage of that ethnic group. Scholars posit that the development of ethnic identity typically begins early in life through socialization practices and customs, but becomes most noticeable during adolescence and young adulthood when individuals begin to develop their own personal and social identities, independent from their parents and other family members (Ortiz and Santos, 2009; Phinney, 1990, 1996, 2001).

In general, research has suggested immigrant college students constantly reconstruct their identities. For example, Jaret and Reitzes (2009) investigated how college student identities and ethnic identities vary among Black, White, and Asian students and among first-, second-, and third-generation students. They used survey data from a sample of 665 students attending a large, diverse, public urban university to create new indexes for several dimensions of college and ethnic identity. By employing existing self-esteem and efficacy indexes to compare Black, White, and Asian students, as well as immigrant-origin students, these researchers found that Whites ranked lower than Blacks on college identity indexes, first-generation immigrant students had higher rankings than subsequent-generation students, and that construction of racial-ethnic identity was related to self-esteem, efficacy, and academic performance.

A growing body of literature on this theme has addressed the negotiation of identity in other dimensions, such as religious participation. Using data gathered from field research in a variety of ethnically diverse campus ministries, Kim (2004) looked at the reasons why second-generation Korean Americans who could easily participate in pan-ethnic, multiracial, or predominately White campus ministries instead chose to participate in separate ethnic campus ministries. Findings indicated that second-generation Korean students had more opportunities to participate in separate religious organizations than pan-ethnic, multiracial religious organizations on campus. These students tended to associate themselves with those who were similar to them in ethnic and religious affiliations. They viewed themselves as a marginalized minority group on campus as they shared experiences of intergenerational conflicts and living in immigrant families in the United States.

The (re)construction of racial and ethnic identity plays an important role in shaping the overall development of college students and their educational experiences in higher education. Several scholars stress the importance of identity development in social contexts (see Gergen, 1991; McEwen, 2003). Individuals' interactions with their environment affect their perceived identities and impact their sense of self and relations with others. Immigrant college students face a myriad of adaptation involving their culture of origin, the culture of the new country, and racism (Berry, 1997; Rumbaut, 1994). For instance, Kim (2010) found that forming and (re)defining identity was a complex and continually evolving process among Asian, Latino, and African (foreign-born) immigrant groups. These students' narratives suggest that they faced the challenge of (re)establishing their identities once starting college. Immigrant students employed three major categorizations when identifying themselves: (1) ethnic immigrant (Asian immigrant), (2) national identity (African immigrant), and (3) American, though wrestling with maintaining or weakening their original national identity (Latino immigrant). Surprisingly, the most common theme that emerged from this analysis of students' perceptions of racial and ethnic identity was the divisions within ethnic groups, particularly between 1.5 (foreign-born who immigrated to the United States at school age or during adolescence) and second-generation (U.S.-born with at least one immigrant parent) immigrants. In many cases, 1.5-generation immigrant students felt a greater divide from second-generation immigrants of their own ethnic group than with any other ethnic group, nonminority or Whites. Kim's study suggests that eliminating stereotypes of certain ethnic groups is critical to dispelling myths that characterize immigrant students as high academic achievers, as well as to alleviating fears these students have as to the fulfillment of college expectations and general college survival.

Based on multiple interviews with three second-generation Black male students at a predominantly White institution, Baber (2011) explored the development of racial identity in Black immigrant students. His study revealed that while second-generation Black male students' racial identity was firmly shaped by parents' national origin identity, these students simultaneously developed a positive sense of self as Black Americans. Although the study's findings were based on only three students' interview responses, it still suggests the need to study varied racial experiences within Black American students.

Racial and ethnic identities and discrimination, among other social and economic considerations, are often acknowledged as major factors in scholarly discussions of the influences on immigrant students' academic success. Yoo and Castro (2011) examined Asian American college students' perceptions of racism and their impact on the academic performance. A sample of 155 Asian American college students from a large university in the Midwest participated in the study. Using hierarchical multiple regression analysis to test main and interaction effects between perceived racism, nativity status, and academic performance, the researchers found that perceived racism was negatively associated with academic performance (measured by cumulative GPA) for foreign-born Asian Americans, while perceived racism increased the academic performance of U.S.-born students. Nativity was used (foreign-born versus native-born) to characterize the Asian immigrant student population in this research. The study suggests that immigration characteristics are important in understanding Asian American college students' experiences of racism and academic performance. In short, links seem apparent between immigrant students' attitudes toward racial and ethnic identity and their collegiate experiences and academic outcomes. Additional research efforts should be made to provide useful frameworks for a greater understanding of the cultural attitudes of diverse groups of immigrant college students, and how these individuals might approach adaptation and identity in college. We should be asking, how do different racial/ethnic immigrant students negotiate a bicultural space, learn to become both immigrant and American, and develop a sense of self "in relation to those around them, based on their social similarity or dissimilarity with the references that most directly affect their experiences"? (Rumbaut, 1994, p. 754).

Career Aspirations and Development

Although past research has found that immigrants' career choices are strongly influenced by parental pressure (Leong and Gim-Chung, 1995), racial prejudice (Lee, 1994), and cultural values (Sodowsky, 1991; Sodowsky, Kwan, and Pannu, 1995), new literature on career aspirations and development among immigrant college students has been relatively scarce. Overall, literature points to generational status, environmental factors, perceived prejudice, acculturation, and parental influence as being associated with students' career choices and aspirations.

Corey (2000) explored the career aspirations of first-generation and second-generation Asian American college students by measuring acculturation and sense of prejudice. A total of 139 Asian American students participated in the study. Results indicated that Asian immigrant parents encouraged their children to pursue careers in science and technical fields to attain prestige and socioeconomic mobility. Second-generation students were more likely to experience frustration with their parents by making career choices that did not meet their parents' expectations. However, first-generation students indicated a higher likelihood of pursuing science careers than second-generation students.

In a study examining the role of parental involvement in the college transition experiences of Chinese 1.5 and second-generation college students, Louie (2001) found that regardless of socioeconomic status, Chinese immigrant parents expect their children to obtain a bachelor's degree and to pursue careers in technical fields. However, she did argue that there are marked differences between middle- and working-class Chinese immigrant parents in the allocation of educational resources to facilitate their children's educational opportunities and social mobility, highlighting the role of social class and ethnicity in immigrant students' career decisions.

Another study examining college major preferences among Asian Indian immigrant college students and their parents, Roysircar, Carey, and Koroma (2010) found that Asian Indian immigrants' generational status, acculturation, perceptions of prejudice, and degree of parental influence were strongly related to their preferences for particular college majors. Second-generation

Asian Indian immigrants reported lower preferences for science majors, higher engagement with the mainstream American society, and lower perceived prejudice than first-generation Asian Indian immigrant students. Similar to Louie (2001), Roysicar, Carey, and Koroma (2010) highlight that parents' perceived prejudice and preferences for science and math were instrumental in second-generation immigrants' inclinations toward choosing these majors, affirming previous research that suggests parents and family are one of the most powerful influences on vocational behavior and career development (see Brown, 2004; Inman, Howard, Beaumont, and Walker, 2007; Sodowsky, 1991; Whiston and Keller, 2004).

Stebleton (2010) examined career development in seven Black sub-Saharan African immigrant adult students attending an urban public four-year university in the Midwest. Using semistructured interviews, he found that sociopolitical and cultural factors in the homeland and ties with family and community were important to career development among these students. After the African students immigrated to the United States, their identities as students and workers evolved. This study is useful in that it focuses on an immigrant student subgroup that has been largely ignored in the literature (Black African immigrants) and provides recommendations for career development practitioners.

In summary, research literature on immigrant college students' career aspirations and development has been scant—the majority of past studies on the immigrant population's career choices and development have focused on adolescents, adult immigrants, or Asian ethnic groups. Although limited, the literature does indicate that immigrant parents act as critical providers of traditional and cultural values for their children and greatly influence their career choices. Given that career aspiration and development is antecedent to the socioeconomic mobility immigrants hope to gain, more attention must be focused on systematically examining how individual attributes (personal characteristics and goals), cultural value orientation, immigrant status, labor market condition, and immigration trends shape immigrant college students' career decisions and trajectories across different racial and ethnic groups.

Conclusion

The main purpose of this chapter was to synthesize research related to immigrant students' multifaceted collegiate experiences, whether academic, psychosocial, or cultural. Although we have sought to look at the multilayered educational experiences of immigrant students using four existing bodies of literature, we acknowledge that these research themes are not exhaustive, but rather are interrelated and interdependent. The intersection of academic, psychological, and socio-cultural adjustment/development shapes the overall student collegiate experience. As well, this review was, to a large extent, shaped and limited by existing research literature.

It is worthwhile to note that across the four overarching research themes addressed here, relationships with parents and peers, interaction between individuals and the (college) environment, emotional and financial support, and immigrant status were important factors influencing immigrant educational experiences. For example, college students from immigrant families often need to negotiate the American higher education system and establish a positive trajectory of achievement without the benefit of having parents with knowledge of this system (Cooper and others, 2002). These students are also likely to be members of ethnic minority groups on whom the dominant society often projects negative stereotypes and diminished expectations (García Coll and Magnusson, 1997). In addition, a sense of family obligation among immigrant students can both encourage and thwart postsecondary educational progress as students feel a sense of duty to contribute financially to their family as well as pressure to succeed academically. The interplay of race/ethnicity, immigrant status, and socioeconomic status affects the college persistence and educational attainment of immigrant students on the postsecondary level.

This chapter also points to a substantive gap in our understanding of race, ethnicity, immigrant status, gender, age at immigration, and context variables (immigration trends, institutional and public policy). Aggregate data does allow us to understand much about immigrant students' high motivation and positive trajectory of academic achievement, transition to postsecondary education, and degree attainment; the demographics of immigrant participation in postsecondary education seem quite robust, with variations in immigrant generational status, country of origin, socioeconomic status, race, and ethnicity. However, the question as to whether immigrant students—either first- or second-generation, low-income, first generation in their families to attend college, or undocumented—are able to succeed educationally beyond the high school years remains yet to be answered. The next chapter addresses undocumented students and their access to college and experience in higher education.

Undocumented Students and Higher Education

A N ESTIMATED 10.8 MILLION UNDOCUMENTED immigrants reside in the United States as of 2010 (Hoefer, Rytina, and Baker, 2010). In the United States, undocumented immigrants made up 28 percent (10.8 million) of the foreign-born population, about 3.7 percent of the entire population, and 5.1 percent of the workforce in 2010 (Passel and Cohn, 2011). It is notable that the undocumented immigrant population is larger now than at any other time since the early twentieth century. Approximately 47 percent of the nation's undocumented immigrants have arrived since 2000, and this population has been at the epicenter of the national immigration policy debate over the past decade (Suárez-Orozco, Yoshikawa, Teranishi, and Suárez-Orozco, 2011). Although the number of undocumented immigrants in the United States is currently below 2007 levels (12 million), it has tripled since 1990 and grown by a third since 2000 (Passel and Cohn, 2011).

Of those undocumented immigrants, an estimated 1.2 million (11 percent) are under eighteen years of age, and 1.3 million (12 percent) are between eighteen and twenty-four years of age (Hoefer, Rytina, and Baker, 2010). The majority of these children and young adults have lived in the United States for at least five years and have received or will receive the bulk of their elementary and secondary education in the United States (Gonzales, 2007). These individuals view themselves as Americans; they have limited, if any, recollection of, or desire to return to, their home countries (Gonzales, 2007; Oliverez, 2006; Perez, 2009).

Of the 80,000 undocumented students who are eighteen years of age, only 50,000 to 65,000 will graduate from high school each year (Passel, 2003). For many of these students education ends at the high school level because a lack of legal status bars admission to a postsecondary institution and/or eliminates the possibility of receiving federal or state financial assistance to cover the costs associated with college attendance (Passel, 2003). Although many of these students are college ready (Oliverez, 2006; Perez, 2009), only a small percentage apply to and attend postsecondary institutions. For example, in 2003, only an estimated 13,000 undocumented students enrolled in postsecondary institutions (Passel, 2003). Even after the passage of tuition equity legislation in twelve states,[7] which permits undocumented students who meet certain criteria to pay in-state resident tuition rates at public postsecondary institutions, the number of undocumented students attending postsecondary institutions has not risen appreciably (Fry, 2002; Gonzales, 2007, 2009). Although passage of tuition equity legislation has opened the doors of higher education for undocumented students, the lack of federal and/or state aid has made it, at best, financially difficult for a large percentage of undocumented students to move beyond a high school education.

In the twenty-first century's global economy, workers need to constantly acquire new skills and training beyond what is taught in high school. The completion of a postsecondary education is now an expectation, not just for social and economic mobility, but also to compete in today's job market (Hunt and Tierney, 2006). According to James B. Hunt and Thomas J. Tierney, over the past quarter century, two groups of citizens have failed to improve their economic status: those who only have a high school education and those who never completed secondary education. Within these groups, a particular subgroup of underserved individuals faces massive challenges in acquiring the higher education needed to compete in a knowledge-based economy and to improve individual socioeconomic status as well as that of family members: the undocumented immigrants. While policymakers and leaders in higher education, as well as state and federal governments, have successfully taken action to increase access for traditionally underrepresented minority groups, first-generation who attend college first in their family, and women, such has not been the case, nationwide, for undocumented immigrants. This "locking out" of a population from higher education is of concern since the population's completion of a postsecondary education is critical to a nation's economic and democratic vitality (Lumina Foundation, 2009). It is estimated that between the years 2010 and 2020, immigrants and their children are expected to make up the majority of the U.S. workforce (Toossi, 2012). The occupations that will be in highest demand during this time period will require an associate's degree or above (Carnevale, Smith, and Strohl, 2010; U.S. Bureau of Labor Statistics, 2010). Therefore, investing in the postsecondary education of undocumented students is important for the social, economic, intellectual, and psychological well-being of these students, and the community at large (Gonzales, 2007).

In this chapter, we attempt to provide general background information on the undocumented population, review federal legislation that has had an effect on undocumented students' admission to and/or financing of a public college education, and discuss state legislation that attempts to address the issue of public higher education for undocumented students.

Background on Undocumented Immigrants

In the past, the majority of undocumented immigrants have lived in the southwestern part of the United States, where Mexicans and South Americans made up the largest group of unauthorized immigrants (Passel, 1999). However, in recent years the ethnic/racial characteristics of the unauthorized immigrant, as well as the areas where they live, have changed (Hoefer, Rytina, and Baker, 2010). Today, the largest percentage of undocumented immigrants is from North America (Mexico, Canada, the Caribbean, and Central America—8.5 million) with 6.7 million Mexicans comprising the majority of unauthorized immigrants, followed by Asia (1 million, primarily from China, India, South Korea, and the Philippines), and South America (700,000) (Hoefer, Rytina, and Baker, 2010; Passel and Cohn, 2011). While California and Texas remain the leading states of residence for undocumented immigrants with an estimated 23.4 percent and 16.4 percent of undocumented immigrants, respectively (Hoefer, Rytina, and Baker, 2010), nontraditional immigrant states, such as Georgia, Virginia, Maryland, Alabama, and North Carolina, are now home to a growing number of unauthorized immigrants (Passel and Cohn, 2011).

The undocumented immigrant population faces discrimination and hostility on a daily basis due to the negative image of undocumented immigrants in the U.S. news media, and anti-immigrant groups continue to perpetuate incorrect information that vilifies these people. This population has been accused of straining state social services, not paying taxes, engaging in criminal activities, and taking jobs away from U.S. citizens, despite evidence that less than 1 percent of immigrants move to the United States for social services (Massey, Durand, and Malone, 2002), are less likely than U.S. citizens to use public services (Nadadur, 2009), contribute to a state's treasury through the payment of taxes (Lipman, 2006), benefit the nation's economy (Soerens and Hwang, 2009), and are less likely than U.S. citizens to commit crimes (Butcher and Piehl, 2008). Not only do these negative perceptions result in hate crimes[8] or discriminatory acts[9] against undocumented immigrants, they create challenges and barriers for undocumented students, who are guaranteed a free public K–12 education under *Plyer v. Doe*.[10] Although undocumented immigrants face barriers in their quest for a college education (Gonzales, 2007, 2009; Rincon, 2008), undocumented students in higher education have exhibited academic resilience (Muñoz, 2008; Oliverez, 2006; Perez and others, 2009) and have achieved academic success in spite of financial difficulties and personal challenges (Albrecht, 2007; Cortes, 2008; Jauregui, 2007; Perez and others, 2009).

Federal Legislation and Undocumented Students

The first piece of federal legislation to affect undocumented students' access to postsecondary education was the Higher Education Act of 1965. While this act provides citizens, legal permanent residents, asylees, and refugees with the possibility of federal financial aid to help pay tuition and fees associated with attendance at a two-year and/or four-year postsecondary institution, undocumented students are denied the opportunity to apply for federally funded loans and grants. Given the fact that 39 percent of undocumented students live below the federal poverty line (Frum, 2007), the denial of federal financial aid has a significantly negative effect on the undocumented student's choice of institution, his or her ability to attend a postsecondary institution, and/or to finance his or her college education (Oliverez, 2005, 2006; Romero, 2001).

In 1996, Present Clinton signed into law the Illegal Immigration Reform and Immigrant Responsibility Act (IIRIRA), which has had a significant impact on undocumented students' admission to and financing of college. Section 505 of the IIRIRA states in part that:

> . . . an alien who is not lawfully present in the United States shall not be eligible on the basis of residence within a state ... for any postsecondary education benefit unless a citizen or national of the United States is eligible for such a benefit (in no less amount, duration, and scope) without regard to whether the citizen or national is such a resident.

The statute does not prohibit states from admitting undocumented students to public colleges or universities or granting in-state resident tuition rates to undocumented immigrants as long as U.S. citizens are afforded the same opportunity (Olivas, 2004; Ruge and Iza, 2004). However, the vagueness of the statute has resulted in states taking divergent approaches to the admission of undocumented students to public postsecondary institutions, as well as the granting of in-state resident tuition rates to this student population (Frum, 2007).

At the same time, the Personal Responsibility & Work Opportunity Reconciliation Act of 1996 (PRWORA), a welfare reform statute that denies public benefits to immigrants who are not legal permanent residents, was enacted. Section 1621 of the PRWORA provides in part that:

> . . . an alien ... is not eligible for any State or local public benefit. ... The term state or local public benefit means ... any retirement, welfare, health, disability, public or assisted housing, education aid, or food assistance, unemployment benefits, or any other similar benefit for which payments or assistance are provided to an individual, household, or family ... by an agency or state or local government.

While the PRWORA specifically denies undocumented immigrants postsecondary aid, it has been generally interpreted as dealing with *federally funded* financial aid, not the prohibition of admission of undocumented students or the awarding of state-funded financial aid (Olivas, 2004; Ruge and Iza, 2005). As with the IIRIRA, some states, such as Alabama and South Carolina, have interpreted this statute as prohibiting undocumented immigrants from enrolling in a public postsecondary institution and/or receiving state-funded financial aid.

The misinterpretation of these two pieces of federal legislation at the state level has had an enormous impact. In all but twelve states,[11] undocumented students are charged out-of-state tuition rates regardless of their length of residence within the given state. These out-of-state tuition rates may be three to seven times the average in-state tuition paid by state residents (Dougherty and Reid, 2007; Frum, 2007; Olivas, 2004; Oliverez, Chavez, Soriano, and Tierney, 2006). For example, in 2009, the North Carolina State Community College Board voted to grant undocumented students access to the state's community colleges. However, the board did not grant undocumented students in-state resident tuition rates. While the 2011 in-state tuition rate at North Carolina's community colleges was $66.50 per credit hour ($1,064.00 maximum per semester), out-of-state tuition was $258.00 per credit hour ($4,136.00 maximum per semester). The undocumented students' ineligibility for federally funded financial aid and inability to seek legal employment as established by the Immigration Reform and Control Act of 1986,[12] and the denial of state-funded aid in all but three states[13] makes it, at best, difficult for undocumented students to defray the high costs of higher education (Perry, 2006), to move beyond a high school education, and to reap the social and economic benefits conferred by a college education.

In 2001, federal legislators introduced the bipartisan Development, Relief, and Education for Alien Minors (DREAM) Act in an effort to rectify the negative effects of the IIRIRA and PRWORA on undocumented students. Passage of the DREAM Act would potentially affect an estimated 45,000 high school graduates every year (National Immigration Law Center, 2006). The initial version of the DREAM Act sought to repeal Section 505 of the IIRIRA, thereby removing any doubt over a state's ability to determine residency for higher education purposes and providing a path to legal residency for undocumented students of good moral character who graduated from a high school in the United States, were under the age of sixteen years at the time of entry into the United States, had resided in the United States for a period of at least five years prior to the passage of the DREAM Act, were accepted at a college or university, and completed, at minimum, an associate degree or served in the U.S. armed forces (Boggioni, 2009). Since passage of the DREAM Act would confer upon eligible undocumented students conditional legal residency, undocumented students would then be eligible to receive federal and state-funded financial aid. Further, the students would be permitted to work and to obtain a driver's license, thereby allowing them to effectively finance their education (Lopez, 2005). The bill did not pass.

Since its first introduction in 2001, multiple versions of the DREAM Act have been introduced into Congress. The most recent version of the DREAM Act (S. 952 and H.R. 1842) was introduced in the 112th Congress on May 11, 2011. The 2011 DREAM Act provided undocumented students with the opportunity to legalize their immigrant status in two steps. The first step, which would change the students' status to conditional residency for a period of six years, requires potential beneficiaries to have entered the United States at the age of fifteen years or younger; have been continuously present in the United States; have good moral character; be admitted to a postsecondary institution or have earned a GED or diploma in the United States; be younger than thirty-five years of age at the time of enactment; and, if male, to have registered with selective service. After six years, the students would be able to remove this conditional status and become legal permanent residents by proving good moral character and continuous residency; acquiring a postsecondary degree or completing a minimum of two years in a bachelor's degree program or serving in the armed forces for two years (S-952; H.R. 1842). Although students qualifying under the DREAM Act would be eligible to receive Ford and Perkins loans, as well as federal work-study, they would not be eligible to receive federally funded grants or scholarships (Bruno, 2011). It is believed that if this version of the DREAM Act had passed, an estimated 2.1 million individuals would qualify for conditional immigrant status (Bruno, 2011; Batalova and McHugh, 2010) with a potential of 825,000 individuals achieving legal permanent residency (Batalova and McHugh, 2010). As of this writing, the act has not passed. However, as recently as June 15, 2012, the Obama administration announced an executive order that stops the deportation of young undocumented immigrants and provides them with work permits (also known as "Deferred Action for Childhood Arrivals" program), but does not grant a path to permanent legal status. The executive order will apply to illegal immigrants who came to the United States before they were sixteen years of age and are younger than thirty years of age, have lived here for at least five years, and are in school, high school graduates, or military veterans in good standing. According to the Pew Hispanic Center (Passel and Lopez, 2012), as many as 1.7 million immigrants (representing about 15 percent of the unauthorized immigrant population in the United States) might benefit from this new policy. Outcomes of this new measure remain to be seen.

State Approaches to Undocumented Students and Higher Education

In an attempt to address the issue of educational opportunities for undocumented students, twelve states have passed legislation granting undocumented students access to public postsecondary institutions at an in-state tuition rate (National Conference of State Legislators, 2011) if certain requirements are met. These requirements are similar in that tuition equity legislation requires the student to have attended a high school within the respective state for a certain number of years and to have graduated from a state high school or obtained a GED. In addition, the State Higher Education Governing Board in Rhode Island adopted a policy granting undocumented students the benefit of paying in-state resident tuition rates, while the Community College System in North Carolina granted undocumented students access to public community colleges at out-of-state rates (see Figure 6).

As a result of in-state tuition legislation passed by state legislatures, the estimated number of undocumented students attending college has increased nationwide (Flores, 2010). Chin and Juhn (2007) have explored the effects of in-state resident tuition policies on the enrollment of undocumented students in public colleges and universities. Using data from the 2001–2005 American Community Surveys and the 2000 U.S. Census, they concluded that the policies had a positive, but minimal, effect on the college attendance of Mexican males aged twenty-two to twenty-four years. Shortly thereafter,

FIGURE 6
State Approachtes to Undocumented Immigrant Students in 2011

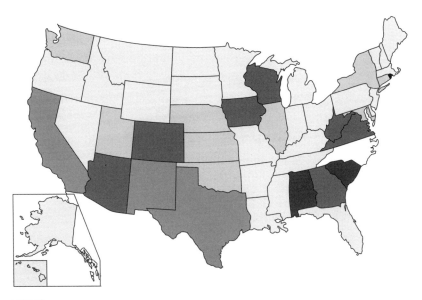

Legend:

	Notes
	North Carolina Community College System grants undocumented students access to public community colleges at out-of-state tuition rates
	No statewide legislation on access or in-state resident tuition rates for undocumented students
	Provides undocumented students with in-state resident tuition rates
	Provides undocumented students with in-state resident tuition rates and state-funded aid
	Provides undocumented students with out-state resident tuition rates
	Denies undocumented students in-state resident tuition rates
	Rhode Island Higher Education Governing Board grants undocumented students in-state resident tuition rates

Sources: National Conference of State Legislatures (2011); National Immigration Law Center (2011); and Russell (2011).

Kaushal (2008) looked at the enrollment and educational attainment of undocumented Mexican immigrants at public postsecondary institutions before and after implementation of in-state tuition policies. Using the Current Population Surveys from 1997 to 2005, Kaushal concluded that in-state tuition policies in California, New York, Texas, and Utah resulted in a 31 percent increase in college enrollment rates.

Recent quantitative studies have provided further evidence for the positive effects in-state tuition policies have had on the enrollment of undocumented students. Flores and Horn (2009) examined the effect of the in-state resident tuition policy on persistence rates of undocumented students enrolled in a selective public institution in Texas as compared to their counterparts (Latino U.S. citizens and legal residents). Their study indicated that undocumented students who were eligible for the in-state resident tuition rates were as likely to stay in college as their counterparts. Flores (2010) explored whether undocumented Latino students living in states with in-state tuition policies were more likely than undocumented students living in states without in-state tuition policies to enroll in a public institution of higher education. Using data from the Current Population Survey and the U.S. Bureau of Labor Statistics for the years 1998 to 2005, Flores found that in-state resident tuition policies have a positive, significant effect on the college enrollment rates of undocumented Latinos. Dickson and Pender (2010) examined the effects of an in-state tuition policy for undocumented students at five public universities and one private in Texas. By comparing the difference in enrollment yields for undocumented students at the six Texan universities before and after implementation of the in-state tuition policy, Dickson and Pender found enrollment rates increased significantly following the implementation of in-state tuition policies, ranging from a 14 percent increase at selective universities to 41 percent at universities with a higher enrollment of Latinos. In addition, they found that in-state policies also reduced the number of Latino high school dropouts.

Qualitative researchers have also begun to document the effects in-state tuition policies on the college experiences of undocumented immigrants. Education is an important goal for undocumented immigrants and in spite of discrimination, barriers, and personal issues faced by undocumented students, they are persisting (Albrecht, 2007; Cortes, 2008; Jauregui, 2007). De Leon (2005) studied the resiliency of ten undocumented Mexican males enrolled in a postsecondary institution in Texas. Focusing on freshmen with fewer than five years of residency in the United States, De Leon found that despite the students' constant fear of being "outed" as undocumented, their uncertainty about their future due to their inability to legally find employment in their chosen field, and the lack of encouragement received from teachers and professors, the students persevered. Family and culture played a strong role in these students' college persistence. De Leon suggested that if these students were provided with financial aid and permitted to find legal employment support, more undocumented students would successfully start and complete a postsecondary education, improve the lives of their families, and contribute to the growth of their communities, society, and the nation as a whole.

Muñoz (2008) studied the college persistence of undocumented female Mexican students attending the University of Wyoming. She found that family and culture played a positive role in the students' college persistence and their immigration experiences gave them a sense of purpose. Students understood the sacrifices their parents made to provide them with a better life, and this understanding provided the students with motivation to succeed. In another study of the critical race narratives of ten female Mexican students enrolled in a research-intensive university, Huber (2009) found that Latina undocumented students utilized various forms of capital including personal, family, and community resources while navigating the college career. This study argues that undocumented students should be given educational opportunities to work toward creating better conditions for themselves and their communities.

Perez Huber and Malagon (2007) examined the college experiences of six undocumented Latino college students in California. They found that these undocumented students identified financial support as the greatest obstacle they faced in college. Ineligibility for federal and state financial aid, coupled with the inability to be legally employed, challenged students' ability to finance postsecondary education. As a result of the restrictions placed on their lives due to undocumented immigrant status, the students expressed feelings of isolation, fear, and invisibility. Perez (2010) examined the college choice of fourteen undocumented Latino students of low socioeconomic status attending college in California. The participants identified cost and affordability as the most important factor in choosing a postsecondary institution. As a result, many chose to attend community college, with the intent to transfer to a four-year institution. The students viewed this path as an affordable option to attain a bachelor's degree.

As evidenced by studies on the college experiences of undocumented immigrants, lack of options for financing is a major concern. While in-state tuition policies have helped increase undocumented students' access to post-secondary institutions, increasing tuition and lack of financial assistance, combined with low socioeconomic status and an inability to work legally, have made it challenging for undocumented students to attend a postsecondary institution and achieve a complete education.

Opposition to In-state Tuition Rates for Undocumented Students

Despite the success evident in the increasing number of undocumented students attending colleges and universities in states that provide in-state resident tuition rates to undocumented immigrants, tuition equity legislation has not gone unchallenged. Detractors, such as Kris Kobach and anti-immigrant or immigration restriction organizations, claim that state resident tuition legislation intended to assist undocumented students seeking a college degree is illegal and unconstitutional. Kobach (2007) argues that in-state tuition policies provide unauthorized immigrants with "extremely valuable financial benefits" (p. 498) and create a "well-educated class of illegal aliens who cannot take advantage of their education" (p. 501), while denying those same benefits to U.S citizens who come from out of state. Kobach takes the position that undocumented students are rewarded for breaking federal immigration laws by in-state tuition legislation while foreign students who have entered the United States legally with student visas are punished by having to pay nonresident tuition. Others argue that the state governments are rewarding illegality via taxpayer subsidies, providing incentive for continued illegal immigration (Huang, 2007).

Kobach's claims as to the illegality and unconstitutionality of in-state tuition legislation have been rejected by the courts in two cases: *Day v. Sebelius* (2005) and *Martinez v. Regents of the University of California* (2010). In *Day v. Sebelius*, six U.S. citizen parents of out-of-state students and eighteen college students, together with the anti-immigrant group Federation for American Immigration Reform (FAIR), filed suit at the U.S. District Court against the governor of Kansas and the president of the Kansas Board of Regents challenging the legality and constitutionality of the Kansas in-state tuition law, which granted undocumented students who meet certain requirements in-state tuition rates. The plaintiffs alleged that the Kansas in-state tuition law violated Section 505 of the IIRIRA and the Equal Protection Clause of the U.S. Constitution in that the state statute unlawfully provided more benefits to undocumented students than U.S. citizens with out-of-state residency. The court dismissed the case, finding that the plaintiffs lacked standing since they were unable to prove injury and damages resulting directly from the enactment of the in-state tuition policy. Although the court did not rule on the constitutionality or legality of the Kansas law, it did put forth in its decision that since the postsecondary education of undocumented students was of significant concern to the state, it was within that state's right to address it as it saw fit.

In *Martinez v. Regents of the University of California* (2005), out-of-state U.S. citizens who were attending or had attended public colleges in California sued, claiming that California's in-state tuition law violated federal statutory law (IIRIRA and PRWORA) and the Equal Protection Clause of the U.S. Constitution. The plaintiffs sought reimbursement for the nonresident tuition fees paid as part of their tuition, as well as damages. The California Superior Court dismissed the case, finding that the plaintiffs had no legal standing. After several appeals, the U.S. Supreme Court denied certiorari without an opinion, and remanded the case to the California Supreme Court. The California Supreme Court ruled against the plaintiffs and found that (1) California's in-state tuition statute did not violate the plaintiffs' rights; (2) PRWOVA does not prohibit undocumented students from in-state tuition eligibility; and (3) in-state tuition policies are not unconstitutional. Although the findings of this case are not binding nationwide, it is a first step toward clarifying the vague and controversial language found in PRWOVA and IIRIRA.

Conclusion

Undocumented students face significant challenges and barriers in attempts to obtain a postsecondary education, ranging from the inability to access a college or university due to laws that prohibit their admission to the inability to pay the tuition and fees associated with a college education. Between 2010 and 2018, immigrants are projected to represent the majority of the labor force in the United States. As more and more occupations require a postsecondary education, it is of the utmost importance to provide undocumented students with the opportunity to attend and graduate from a college or a university without the fears and challenges they presently encounter. The nation should not just take steps to ensure the enrollment and completion of a college education for every American citizen who can benefit from such an education (Hunt and Tierney, 2006), it should also provide undocumented students who are college ready and motivated to learn with the same benefits.

While states have focused on issues of college access, in-state resident tuition, and financial aid, the Congress has failed to address these issues through legislation (Flores and Chapa, 2009). Although some states understand the need for and the importance of educating the undocumented population by making public colleges and universities accessible and affordable to these students, states cannot address two important issues: work authorization and legalization. One way to address these two issues is with the passage of a DREAM Act, which would not only open up academia for undocumented students by eliminating §505 of IIRIRA, but would also provide these students with a means to legalize their immigrant status in the long run. By doing so, the country would be preparing qualified workers to meet the demands of the economy as well as allowing undocumented immigrants to improve their socioeconomic status—dual goals of a postsecondary education. In the next chapter, we turn to community colleges. These institutions serve as an entry point to postsecondary education for many immigrants, so we present some suggestions for innovative programs and practices to better educate immigrant students attending community colleges.

Immigrant Students and Community Colleges

BETWEEN THE YEARS 2010 AND 2030, immigrants and their children are expected to make up the majority of the U.S. workforce. Since the occupations that will be most in demand will require an associate's degree or above, many have responded to President Obama's recent community college initiative, which named education the key to the nation's economic recovery and international competitiveness, by calling for community colleges to serve an increasing number of diverse student populations. Community colleges play a vital role in educating disadvantaged and less academically prepared students, including racial and ethnic minorities, low-income students, first-generation college attendees, and adult learners. Serving nearly half (43 percent) of all U.S. undergraduates (U.S. Department of Education, 2012a), community colleges are especially important for immigrants who aspire to fulfill the "American dream" at an affordable price through various academic, noncredit, and enrichment courses (Zeidenberg, 2008) and attract more immigrant students than any other type of institutions (Teranishi, Suárez-Orozco, and Suárez-Orozco, 2011). Given these realities, it is worth focusing our attention on community colleges, since they provide an important venue for "increasing educational attainment, economic productivity, and civic engagement" (Teranishi, Suárez-Orozco, and Suárez-Orozco, 2011, p. 153) among immigrant-origin students.

Community colleges are distinguished from four-year institutions by their open access admissions, affordability, and a wide variety of curricular functions including the development of basic skills such as reading, writing, and mathematics, vocational and technical training for adults, and continuing education for non–degree seekers (Cohen and Brawer, 2003). These institutions have often served as stepping stones to educational and economic opportunities for the recent immigrant population, providing critical pathways to postsecondary education for immigrants and their families (Wisell and Champanier, 2010). Community college offers a practical choice for immigrant students partly because of low tuition, a typically advantageous geographical location (closer to home), increased flexibility in scheduling with evening and weekend classes, and a variety of course and program offerings related to workforce training, computer skills, civic education and citizenship, and family literacy. They also offer assistance with English as a second language and basic adult education at no charge or for a small fee.

While data on immigrant-origin students enrolled in community colleges are limited (Szelenyi and Chang, 2002), in 2003–2004, 25 percent of 6.5 million degree-seeking students in community colleges came from an immigrant background (U.S. Department of Education, 2006). A more recent report by the U.S. Department of Education (2012b) indicates that higher percentages of immigrant (foreign-born) Hispanic and Asian undergraduates enrolled in community colleges (51 percent for Hispanics and 54 percent for Asians, respectively) in 2007–2008, compared with 44 percent of all undergraduates. This statistic mirrors the national trend of Hispanic and Asian Pacific American students' community college enrollment; nationwide, two-thirds of Hispanic students begin their college careers in community colleges (Solórzano, Rivas, and Velez, 2005), and more than 50 percent of APA college students choose to enroll in community colleges (Lew, Chang, and Wang, 2005). As such, community college is perceived by these students as being the most accessible path to postsecondary education, allowing them to attain tangible skills to improve their short-term employment situation (Erisman and Looney, 2007). With this figure in mind, it is imperative that community colleges understand the crucial role they play in educating the immigrant population.

Immigrants' demand for higher education exceeds the capacity of the current community college system. Some colleges are well positioned to serve the diverse immigrant population's educational needs, but many are not prepared to meet those needs, experiencing financial shortcomings due to the recent recession and competing priorities, and putting a lack of effort and funds toward sustaining programs and services (Wisell and Champanier, 2010). Aside from the recent economic downturn, which has forced community colleges to do more with less, the relatively "unwelcoming" situation in several states (for example, Alabama's 2011 immigration law, one similar to Arizona's, that requires schools to determine students' immigrant status) has created additional challenges for community colleges that have in the past advocated an open-door policy for disadvantaged and underserved students.

The recent economic crisis has raised some fundamental questions about how immigrants fare economically and educationally and how they might respond to the economic recession. Although some immigrants have successfully navigated and completed community college, many fail to attain their academic goal (Conway, 2009, 2010; Rivas, Perez, Alvarez, and Solórzano, 2007). Immigrant students who attend community colleges tend to have a lower socioeconomic status and limited English proficiency and are less prepared academically than those who typically enter four-year institutions (Conway, 2009, 2010). Many immigrant students attend school part time and face especially demanding work and family challenges. In addition, they are generally working to adjust to a country that may have significantly different cultural and social norms from their own (Sutherland, 2011; Teranishi, Suárez-Orozco, and Suárez-Orozco, 2011). Thus, our goal in this chapter is to review relevant research on immigrants in community colleges, discuss the evolving role that community colleges play in educating immigrants, and to describe, in some detail, emerging services and innovative programs designed to aid immigrant populations at community colleges.

Relevant Research on Immigrants at Community Colleges

Vernez and Abrahamse (1996) systematically described the educational attainment of (foreign-born) immigrant students at the postsecondary level using a nationally representative sample (High School Beyond longitudinal data set of tenth and twelfth graders in 1980). They compared the educational participation and academic performance of immigrant students to that of their native-born counterparts within each of the four major racial/ethnic groups. Results showed that immigrant students were as likely as native citizens to enroll in postsecondary institutions. However, the Hispanic immigrant group was the least likely to attend college. This finding was consistent with differences in academic achievement across racial/ethnic groups for the native-born. The study also observed that overall immigrant students who pursued postsecondary education were 10 percent more likely than native-born students to enter community college. This finding highlights the important role that community colleges play in providing access to postsecondary education for immigrants.

Ordovensky and Hagy (1998) later expanded on the work of Vernez and Abrahamse by investigating the post–high school experiences of the 1992 high school senior cohort using the National Educational Longitudinal Study (NELS) data set. They looked at how postsecondary enrollment options differed by generational status, hypothesizing that community colleges may play a more significant role in providing access to higher education for immigrants than for native-born students, due in part to their flexibility in course scheduling and a more inclusive campus climate. Additionally, community colleges offer vocational education that may provide more attractive enrollment options for students who want to further their education but are uncertain as to their ability to succeed in traditional academic fields. Results of the study showed a measurable generational effect. Both first- and second-generation immigrants were more likely than native counterpart students to enroll in community colleges.

Because many immigrants settle in metropolitan areas, large urban cities such as New York, Los Angeles, and Miami have a large number of immigrant students in their educational systems (Camarota and McArdle, 2003; Conway, 2010). For example, the immigrant population accounted for 36.4 percent of New York City's population in 2008 (twice the 1970 count) and 43 percent of the workforce (DiNapoli and Bleiwas, 2010). Moreover, 25 percent of its community college students were recent immigrants who had resided in New York for four years or less, 55 percent for eight years or less, and 56 percent of all community college students spoke a language other than English (Bailey and Weininger, 2002).

Using fall 1990 cohort data from the City University of New York (CUNY), Bailey and Weininger (2002) found that there was not much difference in the enrollment numbers for immigrants between two-year and four-year institutions. However, they did find that 82 percent of foreign-born students at CUNY had attended secondary school in the United States, and that immigrants with high school experience prior to immigration were more likely to enroll in a community college. In terms of educational outcomes for community college entrants, foreign-born students earned significantly more credits than native-born students did. In particular, foreign-born community college graduates who attended high school abroad were the most successful; 42 percent of those who subsequently transferred to senior institutions earned a baccalaureate degree, compared with only 35 percent of native-born transferees. Immigrant students with higher levels of education also tended to use community colleges to strengthen their language skills (Bailey and Weininger, 2002). Finally, this study concluded that Asians were more likely to enroll in four-year institutions, while immigrants from Latin America were more concentrated in community colleges.

It should be noted that Bailey and Weininger's study portrayed a slightly different picture from other national studies of immigrant enrollment at community colleges compared with baccalaureate-granting institutions. This difference in findings can be attributed to the fact that the national HBS and NELS data sets captured different subsets of the immigrant population. Previous studies were limited to immigrants entering the country before or while in high school, while the CUNY data set contained information on all foreign-born individuals regardless of the age at which they established residency in the United States.

Conway (2009, 2010) explored the educational aspirations of immigrant and native students in an urban community college in the Northeast. In her study, the sample was divided into four student groups: native students (native students born to native parents); first-generation native students (native students born to immigrant parents); U.S.–high-schooled immigrants (foreign-born students who attended U.S. high school); and foreign–high-schooled immigrant students. The study found that the majority of students kept their major over the six-semester period, but those students who did change majors were much more likely to lower their aspirations, as indicated by changes from a transfer program to a terminal one. Also, the study showed that while the majority of the U.S.–high-schooled immigrant students were required to take remedial courses, these students were more likely than other student groups to seek admission to a four-year institution. In comparison, the foreign–high-schooled immigrant students, in spite of having the strongest high school performance, were more likely to apply to a community college, indicating a mismatch between educational aspiration and academic preparation. The results of this study indicated that overall immigrant students fared well academically compared with their native-born peers. While immigrants may need additional assistance at the beginning of their postsecondary education such as English proficiency skills, they are likely to outpace native-born students as measured by credits earned and GPA, suggesting the efforts to help immigrants gain access to higher education are worthwhile. However, the experience of immigrants is not homogeneous. For instance, Hispanic immigrant students persistently lag behind; whereas Black immigrant students who have completed their secondary education abroad had better persistence rates than any other groups, calling for further examination. Given that this study utilizes a single institution sample with a large enrollment of minority students, a generalization of these results should be made with caution.

Little qualitative research is available on the educational experience of immigrants in community colleges, but there is an emerging scholarship in this area of research. Sutherland's (2011) qualitative study on seven Black (foreign-born) immigrant men in a community college found that family, peers, and community played an important role in these Black male immigrant students' academic achievement. Black students developed their own strategies to cope with institutional obstacles such as being given misinformation and being treated poorly. Once they transferred to a four-year institution, they struggled academically or socially due in part to the mismatch between what the institution expected and what the student expected. Additional research is warranted to examine academic, cultural, social, linguistic, and financial challenges immigrant students encounter while seeking transfer to a four-year institution.

Issues Related to Immigrant Students in Community Colleges

As the number and diversity of immigrants increase, U.S. demographics, including those associated with the student body of higher education, are changing. As such, a large proportion of immigrant students, especially Asians and Hispanics begin their college career at community colleges. However, only limited knowledge is available about the success of immigrant students in community colleges because of a lack of available institutional, state, and national data on these students' educational experiences and outcomes. Although postsecondary education does not guarantee life skills and individual well-being, it is a key determinant of economic success and social mobility. Community colleges have been the primary resources to respond to diverse needs and create opportunities in communities and regions they serve. However, several factors may impede immigrant students' access to and success in higher education, even within the community college system. The literature shows that support for immigrant students at the postsecondary level is often unplanned and not generally recognized as a necessity (Gray, Rolph, and Melamid, 1996). In the following section, the discussion turns toward critical issues related to immigrant students in community colleges, mainly tuition policy, limited English proficiency, and advising and counseling services.

Affordability and Tuition Policy

A considerable difference in tuition and fees between community colleges and four-year institutions has been reflected in student enrollment by socioeconomic status. The average annual tuition and fees of community colleges are less than half that of public four-year colleges and universities for full-time, in-state students and are less than about one-tenth that of private four-year colleges and universities. The average annual tuition and fees at community colleges in 2011 was $2,963, whereas public four-year colleges and universities averaged $8,244, and private four-year colleges and universities charged an average of $28,500 (The College Board, 2011). As a result, in a report by the U.S. Department of Education containing descriptive profiles of community colleges in the United States, the majority of students (44 percent) enrolled in community colleges were from low-income families, whereas only 17 percent were from high-income families (U.S. Department of Education, 2008).

The affordability of higher education remains a critical issue for many, but particularly for low-income students and families from an immigrant background. While naturalized citizens and legal permanent residents, similar to their native-born counterparts, are typically eligible for in-state tuition in public higher education, considerable state-by-state and institution-by-institution variation exists for other immigrant student groups. For example, as discussed in the preceding chapter, undocumented immigrant students are considered to be ineligible for federal aid and most forms of state aid (Gonzales, 2009). The relatively low cost of community colleges has made them quite attractive to many undocumented immigrants, but recent legislation in several states barred undocumented immigrant students from paying in-state tuition or from attending any public postsecondary institution at all (Dougherty, Nienhusser, and Vega, 2010; Flores and Chapa, 2009; Teranishi, Suárez-Orozco, and Suárez-Orozco, 2011). In spite of the long tradition of community colleges providing access to higher education for those who would not otherwise be able to earn a college degree, community colleges in several states seem to have closed their doors to countless students, exacerbating undocumented students' difficulties with further education after completing high school.

Limited English Proficiency (LEP)

More than half of the foreign-born population age five years and older had limited English proficiency (Batalova and Terrazas, 2010). With the size of the immigrant population hoping for improved English language skills, it falls on community colleges to provide language instruction and services to immigrants. Community colleges have been instrumental in providing instruction and other services to ESL learners (Kuo, 1999). ESL programs are the largest and fastest growing programs at many community colleges (Crandall and Sheppard, 2004). For example, ESL is now one of the largest programs at Miami-Dade Community College, and one of the largest ESL programs in the world is located in Santa Monica Community College in California.

There are several types of ESL programs offered by community colleges. Adult ESL programs vary by purpose or programmatic focus. First, there are those designed for ESL adults lacking basic literacy, with certain programs directed toward adult immigrants who were well educated in their home country. Such programs are often tuition-free, short-term, and noncredit; they typically have a narrow focus on fundamental survival language skills, have functional goals, and utilize vocational language combined with obtaining a GED, ESL with GED, and family literacy programs (Blumenthal, 2002; Crandall and Sheppard, 2004). The individuals targeted by those programs encounter a narrowing job market with fewer types of positions available for those with insufficient English skills. Another category of ESL curricula is the Vocational English as a Second Language (VESL) programs established in community colleges in response to local needs. VESL programs attempt to integrate English language skills into vocational subject areas, often using ESL strategies and techniques to teach specific vocational content (Crandall and Sheppard, 2004).

To make ESL programs successful, community colleges face a complex set of challenges, in particular, the wide range of student English language acquisition levels, prior educational experiences, socioeconomic backgrounds, and educational goals (Blumenthal, 2002). In addition, ESL programs may be housed in developmental education departments, English departments, or adult and continuing education units at community colleges. The diversity of ESL student populations and the process of establishing a home for an ESL program within an institution present quite a challenge. Furthermore, student assessment and course placement procedures as well as institutional policies also vary considerably across institutions. In order to understand the backgrounds of ESL students coming to community colleges, and how these backgrounds affect the approaches community colleges may take toward ESL education, we offer the following categories of immigrant students in the community college ESL system.

Adult ESL Immigrant Students. Adult ESL students are immigrants aged eighteen years or older who are enrolled in one of the many types of adult ESL programs offered by community colleges that provide a wide range of services including survival, employment, citizenship, high school equivalency, and further education (Crandall and Sheppard, 2004, p. 2).

Developmental Immigrants (DIs). Community colleges share the largest proportion of developmental (remedial) education—virtually all community colleges offer developmental education. Almost 60 percent of students enrolled in community colleges are required to take at least one year of developmental course work compared to 25 percent of students in four-year institutions (Bailey, 2009). The term *developmental immigrant* refers to a subset of Generation 1.5 immigrant students who come from non-English-speaking backgrounds, have "traits and experiences that lie somewhere between the first- and second-generation" (Rumbaut and Ima, 1988, p. 103), and are more proficient in spoken English than written English; whereas "regular" ESL students are those who are more proficient in written English than spoken English, as many have learned English in language classes in their native countries. Developmental immigrant students live in non-English-speaking households, attended a U.S. high school in which English was used as the medium of instruction, and are still learning English when they enter college. In addition to language skills and academic literacy, they may face a number of non-academic challenges such as family responsibilities like serving as a translator, financial burdens, and the need to work (Goldschmidt and Ousey, 2011).

Advising and Counseling Services

In addition to difficulties with language, other issues of adjustment affect many immigrant students. Often, academic problems are associated with emotional distress related to the process of immigration and acculturation, which can circularly interfere with language acquisition because learning language involves accepting a way of thinking and expressing oneself (see Harklau, Losey, and Siegal, 1999). Cultural differences are reflected in academic expectations as well. Thus, traditional academic advisement and psychological counseling may be particularly helpful to immigrant students, allowing them to discuss educational goals, credentials, opportunities, and adjusting to the new culture. As Brilliant (2000) explains, during the process of acclimation to new surroundings, many newcomers fear losing their identities and connections with their native culture. This fear, in turn, can negatively affect students' academic success and their willingness to learn English. Psychological counseling in the form of one-on-one advising or acculturation groups that meet regularly with counselors can be effective approaches for community colleges to help students during this transition (Brilliant, 2000; Gray, Rolph, and Melamid, 1996).

Although immigrant students report that they appreciate current faculty support, institutions of higher education offer limited support to immigrants in the form of one-on-one faculty attention, financial assistance, counseling services, and language learning courses (Brilliant, 2000). This presents a special challenge to community colleges looking to successfully meet the needs of immigrant students adjusting to new cultural and societal norms. Because cultural differences can affect immigrant students' learning styles, participation in classes, and interactions with faculty and peers, academic counselors frequently advise new immigrants on techniques for studying, note taking, and test taking (Do, 1996). For example, in American culture, feelings and personal events are discussed openly, even in classrooms, which may not be true of many other cultures. Awareness of cultural differences that affect immigrant students can help counselors and faculty focus on the source of the problem. Immigrants who have difficulties with English or who are unfamiliar with the American higher education system may depend on advisors to assist them in filling out application forms and completing financial aid paperwork. Career counseling is another important service for these students, since many immigrants come to the United States in search of economic opportunities and need to work while attending community college. Finally, in conjunction with job advice and occupational placement, immigrant students also commonly seek guidance on issues of health, insurance, housing, and finance management (Ellis, 1995). Collaboration between counselors and ESL/developmental education instructors in team-teaching freshman seminars on these topics at community colleges can greatly aid immigrant students.

Innovative Programs for Educating Immigrants

At many community college campuses that enroll a large number of immigrants, several programs have been specifically developed to serve immigrants' needs. This section introduces one community college's innovative programs, and a community college consortium for immigrant students, both aimed at assisting diverse immigrant populations in developing basic life skills, academic literacy, and knowledge and enhancing their educational, occupational, and social mobility.

Center for Immigrant Education and Training at LaGuardia Community College

The Center for Immigrant Education and Training (CIET), housed under the Division of Adult and Continuing Education at LaGuardia Community College, part of CUNY, provides comprehensive educational and training programs designed to help low-income, non-English-speaking immigrants. The Center offers free ESOL (English for Speakers of Other Languages) classes designed to help immigrant adults meet the challenges of the roles they play as workers, parents, and residents of New York City. The programs combine English classes with services such as career exploration, job training, and referrals for job placement and to community resources.

The CIET English and Civics program is open to all immigrant adults with limited English proficiency. This program helps students learn how to be more effective residents of New York City through problem-solving activities, lessons on local resources and services, and civic education.

The English for Workers program assists low-income, limited-English-speaking adults seeking the English skills needed for a potential career change. This program is funded by the Department of Labor for Temporary Assistance for Needy Families, which helps those whose earnings are at or under 200 percent of the poverty level, who have a minor child, who have been refugees, or who have been permanent residents or citizens for at least five years.

The Family Literacy program is designed for immigrant parents with children in NYC elementary, middle, and high schools. In addition to the language barrier, immigrant parents often face (1) a lack of familiarity of the school system and the NYC Department of Education; (2) a lack of self-confidence in the ability to advocate for their children; and (3) an unfamiliar cultural attitude toward the role of parents in public schools. Classes focus on English skills and computer literacy so parents can participate more effectively in their children's education. Lessons include workshops on the NYC public school system, educational resources available for children, and techniques for helping children to succeed in school. The program teaches immigrant parents the skills they need to be proactive in their children's education, helping them participate in school events and communicate with school personnel, as well as become more productive in everyday language tasks.

CIET is committed to meeting the needs of immigrants by preparing them to enter or advance their careers in various industries; its courses seek to train students to succeed in the American workplace. Training with the center allows students to map a career trajectory, enhance computer literacy, and identify the skills they already possess that may lead to new positions. The "Bridge to Allied Health Careers" courses, for example, are designed to improve the English language skills of immigrants who are interested in and qualified to join the healthcare industry. The program seeks to prepare students for future jobs, volunteer positions, or internships at local health-related agencies. Its curriculum focuses on the development of test-taking skills and a healthcare-related vocabulary, and provides students with knowledge of actual healthcare work opportunities, connecting them with Allied Health courses and training programs, such as Medical Assistant Training, Certified Nurse Aide Training, and similar programs outside the college. Another focus is the introduction and practice of the conversational/soft-skills needed in the healthcare workplace (for additional information, see www.laguardia.edu/ciet/default.html).

The Community College Consortium

The Community College Consortium for Immigrant Education (CCCIE) was founded in 2008 with financial support from the J. M. Kaplan Fund, supported and hosted by Westchester Community College in Valhalla, New York (www.cccie.org). The mission of the CCCIE is to raise awareness of the role community colleges play in providing educational opportunities to immigrants, and to expand the range and quality of programs for immigrant students at community colleges across the country. The consortium is composed of representatives from community colleges that demonstrate a commitment to immigrant education through innovative programs and services. To facilitate the success of immigrant education programs the consortium advocates the following approaches: (1) demonstrating commitment to immigrant education; (2) serving the "whole student" with an integrated, holistic approach; (3) emphasizing evaluation and outcomes; (4) developing immigrant student leadership skills; and (5) facilitating partnerships with community and business organizations. What follows is a detailed description of each key factor (Community College Consortiums for Immigrant Education, 2011).

Demonstrating Commitment to Immigrant Education. Community college leaders should exhibit their interest in the education of immigrant students by articulating a clear vision for serving these students and developing resources to make that vision a reality. Programs can be strengthened by linking these program goals to the college's overall mission and strategic plan. In addition, building organizational capacity for innovation and facilitating cross-departmental collaborations and community partnerships is necessary for the successful implementation of strategies at the ground level.

Serving Immigrant Students with an Integrated, Holistic Approach. Support services for immigrant students should employ an integrated approach that serves the student holistically, providing both academic and nonacademic support services. This may be strengthened by increasing coordination and centralization of services, by developing multisector partnerships that provide a continuum of support services, and by building relationships with the community beyond the college.

Emphasizing Evaluation and Outcomes. Community colleges must collect data that measure immigrant student progress in conjunction with intent, and should use those data to improve education programs and services. Programs systematically monitor and effectively assesses students' educational and employment gains, class performance, and certificate and/or degree completion.

Developing Immigrant Student Leadership Skills. Community colleges that choose to provide resources to immigrant students and involve them in campus life build leadership and advocacy skills that help these students become motivated active learners. A diverse immigrant student body enhances the academic and social lives for all students, so colleges need to support advocacy efforts, student government initiatives, and student clubs that promote immigrant integration. They should also provide opportunities for immigrant students to help each other, and the communities in which they live, through peer mentoring, learning communities, and service learning.

Partnerships with Community and Business Organizations. Community colleges maintain diverse partnerships with various stakeholders, including K–12 schools, four-year colleges and universities, adult education centers, community and faith-based organizations, employers, and workforce investment boards. Successful partnerships that serve immigrant students share several characteristics, including an emphasis on regular, face-to-face communications to build relationships and trust among staff members; effective management of each partner's resources and strengths; and a willingness on the part of community colleges to consider new ideas for serving immigrant students—even when those ideas come from outside academic circles.

In addition to the above recommendations, the consortium also identifies promising practices for five target areas: (1) ESL, (2) workforce training/career development, (3) community and employer partnerships, (4) access and support for undocumented students, and (5) citizenship and civics preparation (financial literacy, assimilation series, navigating the legal processes). There is no "one size fits all" approach to designing programs and services to meet the diverse needs of an immigrant student body, but the examples provided by CCCIE colleges illustrate efforts to move beyond isolated pilot projects to more strategically align immigrant education initiatives with other programs and campus units (visit the website for additional information at www.cccie.org/community-college-immigration-promising-practices).

Conclusion

The large influx of immigrants in recent decades has contributed to a shift in the U.S. demographics and labor markets that is becoming increasingly evident. As the demand for higher education accelerates, community colleges' open-access policy has provided valuable opportunities for diverse student populations who would otherwise be left behind. Many immigrants view the community college as an ideal place to learn English, prepare to enter a bachelor's degree program, or receive training to enhance their skill sets and, therefore, job opportunities (Seidman, 1995).

Education has become the vehicle for immigrants to more successfully participate in the labor market and democratic affairs, so the flexibility of the community college has proven to offer great advantages to this population. This chapter has addressed questions of how, and how well, the nation's community colleges have responded to growing immigrant populations on their campuses. Because of community colleges' critical role in promoting social and economic integration, college leaders should focus more attention on issues involving these students. To do so, they should pursue not only descriptive statistics concerning immigrant enrollment and retention, but also attitudinal and needs assessments, evaluations of student outcomes, and measures of the effectiveness of remedial and ESL programs. Such information can help institutions determine whether administration and faculty perceptions of immigrants provide an accurate foundation for future policy and program development.

As such, more studies of immigrants' participation in community colleges would be useful to individuals invested in these colleges, such as presidents, administrators, faculty, and government policy makers, as well as researchers, community leaders, and immigrant students themselves and their families. Given the rapid growth of the immigrant population over the last several decades, there is an increasing call for community colleges to provide access to higher education for these countless newcomers. Although more attention has been paid to immigrant students in community colleges in recent years, there is a clear lack of understanding of these students' educational experiences, calling for greater attention to this field of inquiry (Bailey and Weininger, 2002). Some research areas that merit future consideration include studies of immigrant students' educational achievement within the community college system on national, state, and local levels, and how community colleges can systematically facilitate immigrant populations' academic and career advancement. Recent efforts to create shared expertise and innovative strategies, such as the Community College Consortium for Immigrant Education, make it clear that community colleges must take a leading role in educating immigrants in the coming decades.

Though our discussion here centers around the role that community colleges play in promoting immigrant students' educational and socioeconomic mobility, we recognize that community college is one of many entry points for immigrant students to choose from. There are multiple pathways to and through postsecondary education; community college enables immigrants to develop academic skills, competencies, and cultural knowledge and serves as a transition point for those who plan to later move to four-year colleges and universities. Many of the approaches we suggest for community colleges may apply to four-year institutions as well, and we urge readers to also consider the relevancy and applicability of our suggestions to that context.

Concluding Thoughts

WITH THE PASSAGE OF THE Immigration and Nationality Act of 1965, the character of immigration to the United States has changed in fundamental ways—Latino, Asian, and Caribbean newcomers have supplanted those of European descent as the dominant group. This reconfigured influx of contemporary immigrants, no longer focused single-mindedly on assimilation to the dominant culture, has spurred concerns about adaptation, education, civic engagement, and socioeconomic mobility, as well as appropriate focus and scope for immigration policy. Many immigrants regard a college education as the primary means for socioeconomic advancement and adaptation to American society. Considering the ongoing surge of immigrant-origin students in American higher education, this growing student population deserves much more scholarly attention than it currently receives.

Given the heterogeneity within the immigrant student population, we have sought to provide an overview of immigrant demographics and a conceptual model for the term *immigrant*, key conceptual frameworks for understanding the educational experiences of immigrant students, factors associated with college access and success, a discussion of undocumented immigrants at the heart of policy debates and the indispensable role community colleges play in educating immigrant students. Each of these topics merits a volume of its own. Though our treatments are somewhat cursory, our hope is that this monograph piques readers' interest and sheds light on college access and college-related outcomes of immigrant students to aid researchers, faculty, administrators, and policymakers with a myriad challenges and issues related to optimizing the educational experiences of diverse immigrant student groups.

Suggestions for Future Research

Much more work needs to be done to better understand how to improve immigrants' educational experiences at the postsecondary level and beyond as the growth of the immigrant student population accelerates. Existing knowledge on immigrants in higher education has been limited to aggregated data that masks differences within the population. There is a serious need for data pertaining to the immigrant college student population on national, state, and institutional levels. Clear definitions of immigrant populations are missing, which makes it difficult to fully describe immigrant students' characteristics and needs. Because the existing data are not disaggregated by ethnicity, nativity, generational status, immigrant status, or age at entry to the United States, and typically collapse immigrant groups into the pan-ethnic categories, they mask the wide variations in immigrant students.

Even though diverse immigrant students are increasingly part of higher education, their educational needs have also been indiscriminately aggregated: What does going to college and earning a college degree mean to them and their families? Why are some of these students, who were academically successful in high school, struggling with academic pressures once they enter college? What are the patterns by which they negotiate their identities in relation to their racial/ethnic group membership as they adapt to the new college environment? What issues arise as they socially integrate into the broader college community? Are there perceived stereotypes and threats that influence identity formation and adaptation to a new learning context? What influence does the university have on these students' college success? With these questions in mind, we offer several suggestions for future research that may inform policy and practice.

- Additional quantitative research is warranted using large-scale national data sets such as the Baccalaureate and Beyond Longitudinal Study (B&B), the Beginning Postsecondary Students Longitudinal Study (BPS), the Educational Longitudinal Study (ELS), the High School Longitudinal Study (HSL), the National Postsecondary Student Aid Study (NPSAS), the Cooperative Institutional Research Program's (CIRP) Freshmen Survey, U.S. Census American Community Survey and Current Population Survey to examine factors associated with college choice and college persistence and degree attainment among various subgroups of immigrants. Future research should consider race/ethnicity, class, immigrant status, generational status, limited English proficiency (LEP), and age at immigration.

- Future research should offer richly textured descriptions of immigrant students in different institutional settings.
- To assess the longitudinal progress of immigrant college students, there should be ongoing efforts to collect data on English proficiency, career advancement, immigration settlement patterns, and civic engagement among diverse student groups by race/ethnicity, gender, socioeconomic status (SES), country of origin, and generational status.
- More research is necessary to better understand how each social agent (parents, siblings, peers, faculty, institutional staff, and ethnic community) supports and impacts students' access to college, their adaptation to the college experience and degree completion.
- Further research should be undertaken to track diverse immigrant students' persistence and overall intellectual, psychological, social, and moral development throughout the collegiate career.
- Given the continuing high rates of immigration and the diversity of immigrant groups, comparative ethnographic research is necessary to look at whether ethnicity, culture, SES, generational status, immigration context, residential segregation, assimilation patterns, or other factors may be more relevant for one group than for another.
- Community colleges are well positioned to provide access to postsecondary education and training for immigrants. It may be expected that immigrants, especially recent ones, are particularly concentrated in community colleges. More attention should be paid to immigrant students enrolled in public community colleges or other two-year institutions. More specifically, research is needed to examine what should and can be done better or more often by community colleges to assist the immigrant population in acclimating to the United States, developing more advanced skills and knowledge, and enhancing their educational and career pathways.
- Underrepresented students from native-born racial and ethnic minority groups have been the subject of numerous studies, but minority immigrant

students receive little attention. The misperception that immigrant students are high academic achievers must be dispelled by research and practice that demonstrates the existence of the low-income, first-generation, urban, ethnic group subsets of this population and highlights their needs and barriers to success.

- Researchers and student affairs administrators should focus their attention on the academic and psychosocial developmental issues that immigrant students face and explore possible methods for coping with these issues, as compared with native-born racial/ethnic minorities and White students. Once this population is recognized as a viable group that needs support services, student affairs personnel and institutional staff will be able to more effectively improve the quality of college experience and retention for these students.
- Considering the importance of forms of cultural and social capital such as parental involvement, peer networks, and institutional context, in the process of college enrollment and academic and social adjustment, more research is needed in examining the relationship between immigrant status, socioeconomic class, race/ethnicity, social network characteristics, and college persistence and degree completion.
- With the growing presence of undocumented immigrants in K–12 schools, and the coincident controversy among policymakers, educators, and the public about investing in the education of this population, more research should be conducted on the barriers and challenges these undocumented students face in gaining access to postsecondary education and beyond.

Implications for Policy and Practice

In this monograph, we seek to review and integrate literature on immigrant students' educational experiences and outcomes with particular attention paid to transitions to college and collegiate experiences. This should serve as a starting point for considering the ways in which researchers, policymakers, and practitioners may address the unique challenges facing this student population. This section offers general suggestions for policy and practice that colleges and universities may consider in order to better assist this underserved population.

First, the current practice of categorizing immigrants using only racial classifications, which lack demographic depth, leads to a low awareness of the impact these students have on institutions and contributes to their invisibility and an institutional disregard of their individual educational and psychosocial issues. Given the considerable diversity of socioeconomic background, language, and country of origin within the immigrant population, higher education institutions should collect detailed demographic information on immigrant students (for example, ethnicity, socioeconomic background, age upon arrival, immigrant documentation status, other background characteristics).

Second, immigrant students from low-income families, and students whose parents did not attend college in the United States or their home country may not understand the academic demands of a college education. K–12 and postsecondary systems should work together to align high school and college curricula, ensuring that high school students, their parents/guardians, and their school counselors have information about college entrance requirements and workloads, placement tests, and the costs associated with a college education.

Third, due to variations in financial aid policy for immigrant students across states, individual campuses in partnership with state and federal governments need to make the financial aid process transparent and address the differing needs of various immigrant student groups.

Fourth, colleges and universities must be aware that immigrant students tend to rely on social ties, such as ethnic peer networks on campus or ethnic communities, to navigate the college system. Colleges and universities need to educate their faculty and staff on the obstacles immigrant students face so that they can anticipate students' needs and suggest appropriate interventions. Building positive and meaningful relationships between faculty and students, and administrators and students, is crucial. More systemic approaches, such as formal and informal peer mentoring programs, ethnic cultural centers, and diverse student organizations, should also be developed to assist immigrant students and provide a sense of community.

Fifth, the support and expectations of students' families are key contributors to persistence and success in college. This hints that university personnel should enlist the assistance of parents, other family members, and friends to help immigrant students negotiate the transition process before and during college. Communication with parents, using avenues such as newsletters, can provide parents with an understanding of the important role they play in their children's persistence and success. Culturally sensitive parent orientation programs can also help new students become familiar with the college setting. In addition, the majority of recent immigrant students' parents have lacked English language skills, so bilingual programs for parents should also be considered.

Sixth, the campus environment itself may contribute to certain difficulties for immigrant students. A campus in which faculty and staff promote the customs and values of traditionally White institutions may adversely influence the academic achievement and psychological well-being of this population. University administrators and faculty must be cognizant of ways in which they can promote diversity while eliminating racialized institutional policies.

Finally, a lack of English proficiency in combination with racial discrimination on campus affects immigrant students' adaptation to college. For many immigrant students, limited English skills often accentuate their "foreignness" and resulted in discrimination and hostility. Hence, institutions of higher education should make an effort to hire multicultural and bilingual staff to work more closely with racially diverse and limited English proficient students.

Conclusion

Before public elementary (and later secondary) schooling became compulsory more than a century ago, few native-born citizens and even fewer immigrants dreamed of going to college. Just as the emergence of mandated public schooling in the late nineteenth century coincided with a massive wave of European immigration, so did the explosive expansion of college attendance in the third quarter of the twentieth century coincide with the "new" non-European wave of immigration. The education levels of recent immigrant populations, however, have fallen relative to native-born counterparts, and consequently the average wages of immigrants are now well below those of the native-born population. Amidst today's global expansion of higher education and an increasingly globalized economy that privileges college-educated members of the workforce, many of today's young immigrants and their parents expect not only a high school diploma but also a college degree. The future of higher education and our economy may depend on our ability to address the needs of these diverse immigrant students; more attention must be paid to this student segment than ever before.

Our monograph focuses on issues related to immigrant students by presenting currently available, though always evolving, research and practices. There remains much to learn about how multiple layers of context affect access to postsecondary education and educational outcomes for immigrants, such as the dynamics of race/ethnicity, immigration status, generational status, country of origin, and social class. We acknowledge that one program, one definition, and one policy do not fit all. In order to better understand immigrant students' educational experiences, improve their educational opportunities, and help them become productive and engaged democratic citizens, we need to pay more attention to how public and institutional policy towards admissions and financial aid affect immigrant students. We also need to look at how student affairs policy and practices, as well as institutional academic policies, influence immigrant students' development and growth. The increasingly diverse and multicultural visage of the college community, as well as the growing number of immigrants on college campuses, raises questions as to how, and how well, institutions are helping immigrants adapt to the college environment and achieve their educational goals. To meet the developmental needs of immigrant students, the higher education community must make a concerted effort to increase sensitivity to immigration policy issues and cultural nuances, and become even more creative in their programmatic and intervention efforts to serve the unique set of challenges these students face.

Notes

1. The NPSAS is a nationally representative sample of more than 100,000 students enrolled in U.S. postsecondary institutions. According to the NPSAS, immigrant undergraduates include foreign-born undergraduates who were U.S. citizens with at least one foreign-born parent, resident aliens, and noncitizens eligible for citizenship.

2. Some authors contend that the term *illegal* has negative connotations, while the term *unauthorized* is more neutral and descriptive to refer to those immigrants who live in the United States without legal authorization (Suárez-Orozco, Yoshikawa, Teranishi, and Suárez-Orozco, 2011).

3. In 1960s, Italian-born immigrants made up 13 percent of all foreign-born, followed by those born in Germany and Canada (accounting for 10.2 percent and 9.8 percent, respectively). Unlike in 2009, no single country accounted for more than 15 percent of the total immigrant population in 1960 (Batalova and Terrazas, 2010).

4. The naturalization rate of legal permanent residents may be considered a measure of assimilation and adaptation in the United States. Mexican immigrants have historically had the lowest naturalization rates, whereas Asian immigrants have had the highest naturalization rates (Jiménez, 2011).

5. If readers are interested in an in-depth theoretical discussion and review of literature on cultural capital and social capital in educational research, we recommend Rachelle Winkle-Wagner's (2010) *Cultural Capital: The Promises and Pitfalls in Educational Research*.

6. The term *immigrants with limited English proficiency (LEP)* is used interchangeably with the term *language minority (LM) immigrants* to refer to those who speak a language other than English at home in this volume.

7. The twelve states are Texas, California, Utah, New York, Washington, Oklahoma, Illinois, Kansas, New Mexico, Nebraska, Maryland, and Connecticut.

8. See Costantini, C. (2011, October 17). Anti-Latino hate crimes rise as immigration debate intensifies. *Huffington Post.* Retrieved from www.huffingtonpost.com/2011/10/17/anti-latino-hate-crimes-rise-immigration_n_1015668.html.

9. See Bland, K. (2006). Robotics team finished second. *The Arizona Republic.* Retrieved from www.azcentral.com/families/education/. . ./0703robotics0703.html; and Brennan, N. (2007, Feb, 22). Find the illegal immigrant: College Republicans' event today incites protest from student groups. *Washington Square News.* Retrieved from http://media.www.nyunews.com/media/storage/paper869/news/2007/02/22/News/find-The.Illegal.Immigrant-2736345.shtml.

10. In *Plyler v. Doe* (1982), the Supreme Court struck down a Texas law that withheld funding from school districts that used the funding, in whole or in part, to educate unauthorized children. The Court, in an equal protection analysis, found undocumented immigrants to qualify as "persons" protected under the Fourteenth Amendment and guaranteed a free K–12 public education to all undocumented children. In the 5–4 decision, the Court found no conceivable education policy or state interest that justified the denial of a free public school education to undocumented children who were in the United States through no fault of their own. According to Justice Brennan ". . . for those who reside in the United States with the intent of making it their home . . . it is difficult to understand precisely what the state hopes to achieve promoting the creation and perpetuation of a subclass of illiterates within the boundaries, surely adding to the problems and costs of unemployment, welfare, and crime" (p. 230). The guarantee of a public education for undocumented students does not extend to higher education.

11. Texas, California, Utah, New York, Washington, Oklahoma, Illinois, Kansas, New Mexico, Nebraska, Maryland, and Connecticut.

12. Section 274(a) of the Immigration Reform and Control Act of 1986 provides, in part, that "it is unlawful for a person or other entity to hire . . . for employment in the United States ... an unauthorized alien . . . or to continue to employ the alien in the United States knowing the alien is (or has become) an unauthorized alien with respect to such employment."

13. Texas, New Mexico, and California are the three states granting eligible undocumented students state-funded financial aid.

Appendix: Studies on Educational Experiences of Immigrant College Student Populations

Study	Sample/Participants	Research Design and Methods	Key Findings
College Adjustment and Persistence			
Boureiko (2010)	First- and second-generation immigrant college students (NPSAS:00, 04, & 08)	Quantitative, descriptive statistics, and stepwise regression	Asian and European immigrant students tended to have a higher level of educational attainment than their counterparts from Latin America. The children of those educated immigrants are also more likely to have higher retention and higher graduation rates than their counterparts from families of lower socioeconomic status.
Chen, Gunderson, and Seror (2005)	15 East Asian immigrant students	Qualitative, structured interviews	Contending with the traditional notion of "resilience," the authors argued that the study participants were resilient in that they overcame challenges to learning in English and matriculated in college successfully. A strong cultural belief in the value of education and family support were closely related to the students' resilience.
Crosby (2010)	11 developmental immigrant students (DISs)	Qualitative	The four major themes of identity construction emerged with regard to the use of academic literacy in an academic reading course for DIS in their first semester at university: certain identities, divided identities, transnational identities, and expert identities.

(Continued)

Appendix (continued)

Study	Sample/Participants	Research Design and Methods	Key Findings
Douglass and Thomson (2010)	Over 10,000 UC-Berkeley undergraduates including immigrants	Quantitative, the Student Experience in the Research University Survey of the UC students	Overall, about 28 percent of UC-Berkeley undergraduate respondents reported that they immigrated to the United States. European-American and Chicano students showed higher levels of satisfaction with their academic and social experiences in college than did Chinese students, suggesting a complex set of differences between various "generations" of immigrant students and ethnic backgrounds.
Erisman and Looney (2007)	Multiple data sources (U.S. Census, OIS, and NCES), immigrants with permanent resident status	Quantitative	Twenty-seven percent of all immigrant students and 32 percent of permanent residents in a national sample had attained an associate's degree or certificate, compared with 23 percent of all undergraduates. However, only 23 percent of all immigrant students and 19 percent of permanent residents earned a bachelor's degree, compared with 30 percent of all undergraduates. Further, immigrant students have higher unmet financial needs than the average amount for undergraduate students. Immigrant undergraduate students who depended on their parents for financial support were 86 percent more likely to come from the lowest income quintile than other dependent undergraduate students, and 71 percent of dependent legal permanent residents were in the two lowest income quintiles.

Source	Sample	Method	Findings
Fuligni and Witkow (2004)	650 youth from immigrant families	Quantitative	The immigrant participants demonstrated the same level of postsecondary educational progress as their peers from U.S.-born families in four-year-institution enrollment, persistence, and degree completion. In addition, youth from immigrant families were more likely to support their families financially and were more likely to live with their parents compared to those from American-born families. Variability among immigrant families suggested that youth from families with higher incomes, higher levels of parental education, and East Asian backgrounds were more likely to enroll and persist in postsecondary schooling compared with their peers.
Gonzalez and De La Torre (2002)	A random sample of 5% of Arizona's 3,665,228 resident in April of 1990.	Quantitative, regressions analysis	Overall, the educational attainment rates (secondary and postsecondary education) of Hispanic immigrants were relatively lower than their native White counterparts. Socioeconomic status was found to be an important factor in college completion among Hispanic immigrants.
Heilig, Rodriguez, and Somers (2011)	English learners (ELs) from 50 public universities and colleges to descriptively examine recent enrollment trends in Texas	Quantitative, descriptive	The Texas Top Ten Percent Plan is to increase the number and diversity of students applying for and enrolling in Texas public colleges and universities. If students are in the top 10 percent of their high school class, they are automatically admitted to any public institutions within the state of Texas. Although the large proportion of the top 10 percent ELs enrolled at non-flagship institutions, the top 10 percent plan has increased an enrollment of EL at flagship institutions in Texas.

(Continued)

Appendix (continued)

Study	Sample/Participants	Research Design and Methods	Key Findings
Jenkins, Harburg, Weissberg, and Donnelly (2004)	146 Black female students	Quantitative	Black students whose fathers were foreign-born stayed in college longer than did Black students whose fathers were U.S.-born. Academic performance and placement tests were found to be more predictive for the Black students born to foreign-born father.
Kim (2009)	49 minority 1.5-generation immigrant students from a large public midwestern university	Qualitative, in-depth interviews	Ethnic minority immigrant students tended to rely on peer networks of the same ethnicity rather than on institutional staff when seeking assistance in adapting to the college environment. Ethnic peer network membership on campus contributed to minority immigrant students' adjustment in the first year.
Maramba (2008)	82 Filipina American students	Qualitative	Three primary themes were identified: family/parent influence, home obligations/gender differences, and importance of negotiating their Filipina American identity within the context of their home and college experiences. The study found that Filipina students felt pressure to do well academically in college while maintaining their duties at home. Moreover, their relationships with parents and siblings continued to influence the daily lives of these students on campus.

Museus and Maramba (2011)	143 Filipino Americans/immigrants	Quantitative	Results indicate that the extent to which Filipino college students maintained their cultural values and origin was positively related to their college adjustment experience, pointing to the importance of cultural factors in enhancing minority students' sense of belonging to the campus community.
Nazon (2010)	390 immigrant students in an educational opportunity program, urban, public, four-year institution	Quantitative, chi-square, t-test, and regression analysis	The results indicate that high school GPA was the strongest predictor of college completion among immigrant students who participated in the SEEK educational opportunity program. Household composition, year of entry, and gender were also found to have significant effects on college completion. Other preenrollment variables (for example, age, English as a primary language, and length of residency) did not significantly affect college completion.
Robinson-Wood (2009)	80 Black females (eighteen to twenty-five years old from a private, predominantly White and urban university in the Northeast)	Mixed methods	The results identified five major stressors among Black female students: relationship troubles, academic pressures, inadequate resources, family obligations, and microaggressions.

(Continued)

Appendix (continued)

Study	Sample/Participants	Research Design and Methods	Key Findings
Rocha-Tracy (2009)	149 students, both immigrant and nonimmigrant, at two universities in Boston, one public and one private	Qualitative, interview	Immigrant students adopted many coping strategies to adapt the new college environment including selection of disciplines and professors to work with, building support and social network among students who shared similar difficulties, finding academic support and mentors, and so on.
Stebleton, Huseman, and Kuzhabekova (2010)	55,433 immigrant and nonimmigrant college students	Quantitative, survey	Immigrant students' sense of belonging and satisfaction is significantly lower than that of nonimmigrants. Immigrant college students—whether they arrived in the country as a child, or later as a teenager or young adult, or are the children of parents born outside the United States (second generation)—consistently reported lower levels of sense of belonging and satisfaction compared to their third- or fourth-generation (nonimmigrant) peers.
Sy and Romero (2008)	20 first- and second-generation Latina women, aged eighteen to twenty-nine	Qualitative, semistructured interviews	The authors identified three key themes: (a) the participants emphasized the need to be self-reliant to relieve burden on their family; (b) these women reported that they did not feel obligated to financially support their family, rather their financial contribution was voluntary; and (c) they often felt responsible for taking a parenting role for their younger siblings. This study suggests that more effort is needed to help Latina college students reduce their family obligations and maintain close relationships with family to facilitate adjustment to college.

Tseng (2004)	998 American youth with Asian Pacific, Latino, African/ Afro-Caribbean, and European back-grounds	Quantitative	Asian Pacific Americans emphasized more family interde-pendence than European Americans. Across all pan-ethnic groups, family interdependence was more important to youth with immigrant parents than to youth with U.S.-born parents. A sense of family obligation motivated immi-grant students to do well academically, but they spent more time on meeting the demands of family.
Zajacova, Lynch, and Espenshade (2005)	107 nontraditional, largely immigrant and minority, college fresh-men at a large urban commuter institution	Quantitative, sur-vey, measure the level of academic self-efficacy and perceived stress; structural equation models	Although self-efficacy was a strong predictor of freshman cumulative GPA and credits earned, it did not have a signif-icant effect on predicting persistence in the second year of school among immigrant and minority students. However, stress was negatively related to GPA and the second year persistence.

Psychological Development and Acculturation

Buddington (2002)	150 Jamaican immi-grant college students	Quantitative, survey	Recent immigrants were found not to be highly accultur-ated, indicating a positive correlation between the length of residency and the level of acculturation. Students' accultur-ation was not related to their level of self-esteem or state of depression. Students married to Jamaicans, who returned home to see their relatives and continued to communicate with them had high academic achievement. The frequency of returning home was found to be inversely related to acculturation.

(Continued)

Appendix (continued)

Study	Sample/Participants	Research Design and Methods	Key Findings
Chau (2006)	63 first-generation Chinese immigrant students	Quantitative	The respondents who had a higher level of spiritual well-being reported a lower level of acculturative stress, suggesting that spirituality and religious involvement could be used to cope with acculturative stress among Chinese immigrant college students.
Desai (2006)	218 college students of White and Asian American background	Quantitative, survey	Asian immigrant college students showed greater intergenerational conflict as compared to their White student counterparts. The findings suggested that family therapy might be more effective when working with students from immigrant families.
Huang (2006)	66 Chinese immigrant female college students between the ages of eighteen and thirty	Quantitative, survey	The level of acculturation is negatively correlated to the level of perceived stress, and the level of adherence to Asian cultural values is positively correlated with the level of perceived stress, presenting the possibility of a direct relationship between adhering to Asian cultural values and higher perceived stress levels.

Schwartz, and others (2011)	3,251 first- and second-generation immigrant students from thirty institutions	Quantitative, survey	Results of the study indicated that both first- and second-generation immigrant students engaged in health risk behaviors at similar rates but found racial and ethnic differences in the associations between acculturation and health risk behaviors. For example, among East Asian participants, the adoption of U.S. cultural practices and identification was positively associated with sexual risk taking and with hazardous alcohol use, whereas among Black participants, heritage (native) cultural orientation was negatively related to alcohol use. For Hispanic participants, heritage-cultural practices were negatively associated with sexual risk taking, whereas ethnic identity was positively associated with sexual risk taking.
Tsai-Chae and Nagata (2008)	93 Asian American college students from immigrant families	Quantitative, hierarchical regression models	Findings indicated that the more discrepancies in Asian values between Asian students and their parents, the more parent-child conflict. Asian immigrant students reported they conflicted with their mothers in terms of family norms while they conflicted with their fathers with regard to education/career issues.

(Continued)

Appendix (continued)

Study	Sample/Participants	Research Design and Methods	Key Findings
Social Identity Development			
Baber (2011)	Three second-generation back males	Qualitative	The study revealed that while second-generation Black male students' racial identity was firmly shaped by their parents' national origin identity, these students simultaneously developed a positive sense of self as being Black American. Although the findings of the study were based on only three students' interview responses, this study suggests the need to study varied racial experiences within Black American students.
Benesch (2008)	Generation 1.5	Critical discourse analysis	Generation 1.5 defined as foreign-born who received some formal education in the United States viewed themselves as minorities who experience racism on a daily basis on college campuses.
Brettell and Nibbs (2009)	South Asian American college students (second-generation immigrants)	Qualitative	This study explored the identity construction of Asian Indian second-generation college students. This hybrid identity is constructed through engagement with the ethnic festival on campus and self-reflection on identifying who they were and integrating themselves to the ethnic culture.
Jaret and Reitzes (2009)	665 first-, second-, and third-generation students	Quantitative, survey	Whites are lower than Blacks on college identity indexes, immigrant students are higher than subsequent-generation students, and construction of racial-ethnic identities was related to self-esteem, efficacy, and academic performance.

Kim (2004)	Second-generation Korean Americans	Qualitative, ethnographic	Second-generation Korean students had more opportunities to participate in separate religious organizations than pan-ethnic, multiracial religious organizations on campus. These students tended to associate themselves with those who were similar to them in terms of ethnic and religious affiliations. They viewed themselves as a marginalized minority group on campus and they shared the experiences of having intergenerational conflicts and living in immigrant families in the United States.
Kim (2010)	52 1.5-generation immigrants	Qualitative	Forming and (re)defining one's own identity was a complex and continually evolving process among three ethnic immigrant groups (Asian, Latino, and African).
Yoo and Castro (2011)	155 Asian college students	Quantitative, survey	Perceived racism was negatively associated with academic performance (measured by cumulative GPA) for foreign-born Asian Americans while perceived racism increased the academic performance of U.S.-born students. The study suggests that immigration characteristics are important in understanding the experience of racism and academic performance of Asian American college students. Linkages seem apparent between immigrant students' attitudes toward racial and ethnic identity and their collegiate experiences and academic outcomes.

(Continued)

Appendix (continued)

Study	Sample/Participants	Research Design and Methods	Key Findings
Career Aspirations and Development			
Corey (2000)	139 Asian American students from the University of Nebraska–Lincoln and Creighton University	Quantitative, the Minority-Majority Relations Survey and the Career Aspirations Survey (CAS)	The results confirmed previous research, suggesting that later generations are more likely to acculturate to the United States, and Asian immigrant parents encouraged their children to pursue careers in science and technical fields to attain prestige and socioeconomic mobility. U.S.-born second-generation students were more likely to experience frustration with their parents in career choices that did not meet their parents' expectations. However, foreign-born first generation students indicated a higher likelihood of pursuing science careers than U.S.-born second generation students.
Louie (2001)	1.5- and second-generation Chinese immigrant college students	Qualitative, interview	Regardless of socioeconomic status, Chinese immigrant parents expect their children to obtain a bachelor's degree and to pursue careers in technical fields. However, she argued that there are marked differences in allocating educational resources between middle- and working-class Chinese immigrant parents to facilitate their children's educational opportunity and social mobility, highlighting the role of social class and ethnicity in immigrant students' career decisions.

| Roysircar, Carey, and Koroma (2010) | 139 Asian Indian first- and second-generation immigrant students and 270 parents | Quantitative, survey | Asian Indian immigrants' generational status, acculturation, perception of prejudice, and parental influence were strongly related to their preference for college majors. Second-generation Asian Indian immigrants reported lower preferences for science majors, higher engagement with the mainstream American society, and lower perceived prejudice than first-generation Asian Indian immigrant students. |
| Stebleton (2007) | 7 Black, sub-Saharan African immigrant adult students | Qualitative Hermeneutic, interview | Sociopolitical and cultural factors in the homeland and ties with family and community are important to career development among African students. After the African students immigrated to the United States, their identities as students and workers evolved. This study is useful in that it focused on the immigrant student group that has been largely ignored in the literature (Black African adult immigrant college students) and provided recommendations for career development practitioners. |

References

Alba, R., and Nee, V. (1997). Rethinking assimilation theory for a new era of immigration. *International Migration Review, 31*(4), 826–874.

Alba, R., and Nee, V. (2003). *Remaking the American mainstream: Assimilation and the new immigration.* Cambridge, MA: Harvard University Press.

Albrecht, T. J. (2007). *Challenges and service needs of undocumented Mexican undergraduate students: Students' voices and administrator's perspectives.* (Doctoral dissertation). Retrieved from ProQuest Dissertation and Theses. (UMI 3290814).

Allen, M. L., and others. (2008). The relationship between Spanish language use and substance use behaviors among Latino youth: A social network approach. *Journal of Adolescent Health, 43*(4), 372–379.

Alsalam, N. A., and Smith, R. E. (2005). *The role of immigrants in the U.S. labor market.* Washington DC: Congressional Budget Office.

American Youth Policy Forum. (2009). *Moving English language learners to college- and career-readiness.* Issue Brief. Washington, DC: American Youth Policy Forum.

American Youth Policy Forum. (2010). *Building capacity to promote college-and career-readiness for secondary-level English language learners: Policy brief featuring Austin, Texas.* Washington, DC: American Youth Policy Forum.

Antonio, A. L. (2001). Diversity and the influence of friendship groups in college. *Review of Higher Education, 25*(1), 63–89.

Auerbach, S. (2006). If the student is good, let him fly: Moral support for college among Latino immigrant parents. *Journal of Latinos and Education, 5*(4), 275–292.

Avery, C., and Kane, T. J. (2004). Student perceptions of college opportunities: The Boston COACH program. In C. Hoxby (Ed.), *College decisions: The new economics of choosing, attending and completing college* (pp. 355–394). Chicago: University of Chicago Press.

Baber, L. D. (2011). Bicultural experiences of second-generation Black American males. In R. T. Palmer and J. L.Wood (Eds.), *Black men in college: Implications for HBCU's and beyond* (pp. 89–106). New York: Routledge.

Bailey, T. (2009). Challenge and opportunity: Rethinking the role and function of developmental education in community college. In A. C. Bueschel and A. Venezia (Eds.), *Policies and practices to improve student preparation and success.* New Directions for Community Colleges, Vol. 145. (pp. 11–30). San Francisco: Jossey-Bass.

Bailey, T., and Weininger, E. (2002). *Performance, graduation, and transfer of immigrants and natives in city university of New York Community Colleges.* New York: Columbia University Community College Research Center.

Bankston, C., and Zhou, M. (1997). The social adjustment of Vietnamese American adolescents: Evidence for a segmented-assimilation approach. *Social Science Quarterly, 78*(2), 508–523.

Bankston, C., and Zhou, M. (2002). Being well vs. doing well: Self-esteem and school performance among immigrant and non-immigrant racial and ethnic groups. *International Migration Review, 36*(2), 389–415.

Barker, M. (1981). *The new racism.* London: Junction.

Batalova, J. (2011). *Asian immigrants in the United States.* Washington, DC: Migration Information Center.

Batalova, J., and Fix, M. (2008). *Uneven progress: The employment trajectories of skilled immigrants in the United States.* Washington, DC: Migration Policy Institute.

Batalova, J., and Fix, M. (2011). *Up for grabs: The gains and prospects of first and second generation young adults.* Washington, DC: Migration Policy Institute.

Batalova, J., and Lee, A. (2012). *Frequently requested statistics on immigrants and immigration in the United States.* Washington, DC: Migration Policy Institute.

Batalova, J., and McHugh, M. (2010). *DREAM v. reality: An analysis of potential DREAM act beneficiaries.* Washington, DC: Migration Policy Institute.

Batalova, J., and Terrazas, A. (2010). *Frequently requested statistics on immigrants and immigration in the United States.* Retrieved December 10, 2011, from www.migrationinformation.org/USfocus/display.cfm?ID=818.

Baum, S., and Flores, S. M. (2011). Higher education and children in immigrant families. *Future of Children, 21*(1), 171–193.

Benesch, S. (2008). Generation 1.5 and its discourses of partiality: A critical analysis. *Journal of Language, Identity, and Education,* 7(3–4), 294–311.

Bennett, P. R., and Lutz, A. (2009). How African American is the net Black advantage? Differences in college attendance among immigrant Blacks, native Blacks, and Whites. *Sociology of Education, 82*(1), 70–100.

Bernstein, R. (2007). *Minority population tops 100 million.* Retrieved January 15, 2012, from www.census.gov/dcmd/www/embargo/popest/national/pio-nat_stat.html.

Berry, J. W. (1970). Marginality, stress and ethnic identification in an acculturated Aboriginal community. *Journal of Cross-Cultural Psychology, 1*(3), 239–252.

Berry, J. W. (1980). Acculturation as varieties of adaptation. In A. Padilla (Ed.), *Acculturation: Theory, models and some new findings* (pp. 9–25). Boulder, CO: Westview.

Berry, J. W. (1990). Psychology of acculturation. In J. Berman (Ed.), *Cross-cultural perspectives: Nebraska Symposium on Motivation* (pp. 201–234). Lincoln: University of Nebraska Press.

Berry, J. W. (1997). Immigration, acculturation, and adaptation. *Applied Psychology, 46*(1), 5–34.

Berry, J. W. (2003). Conceptual approaches to acculturation. In K. Chun, P. Balls Organista, and G. Marín (Eds.), *Acculturation: Advances in theory, measurement, and applied research* (pp. 17–37). Washington DC: American Psychological Association.

Berry, J. W., and Sam, D. L. (1997). Acculturation and adaptation. In J. W. Berry, M. H. Segall, and C. Kigitcibasi (Eds.), *Handbook of cross-cultural psychology: Social behavior and applications* (Vol. 3, pp. 291–326). Boston: Allyn & Bacon.

Berry, J. W., Trimble, J., and Olmedo, E. (1986). The assessment of acculturation. In W. J. Lonner and J.W. Berry (Eds.). *Field methods in cross-cultural research* (pp. 291–324). Newbury Park, CA: Sage.

Betts, J. R., and Lofstrom, M. (1998). *The educational attainment of immigrants: Trends and implications* (NBER, Working Paper 6757). Retrieved January 20, 2012, from www.nber.org/papers/w6757.pdf.

Biswas, R. (2005). *Access to community college for undocumented immigrants: A guide for state policymakers.* Boston: Jobs for the Future.

Bitter, C., and Golden, L. (2010). *Approaches to promoting college readiness for English language learners.* Washington, DC: American Institutes for Research.

Blumenthal, A. (2002). English as a second language at the community college: An exploration of context and concerns. In A. C. Bueschel and A. Venezia (Eds.), *Policies and practices to improve student preparation and success* (pp. 45–54). New Directions for Community Colleges, Vol. 117. San Francisco: Jossey-Bass.

Boggioni, J. A. (2009). Unofficial Americans—what to do with undocumented students: An argument against suppressing the mind. *University of Toledo Law Review, 40*, 453–486.

Borjas, G. (2011). Poverty and program participation among immigrant children. *The Future of Children, 21*(1), 247–266.

Bourdieu, P. (1977). Cultural reproduction and social reproduction. In J. Karabel and A. H. Halsey (Eds.), *Power and ideology in education* (pp. 487–511). New York: Oxford University Press.

Bourdieu, P. (1986). The forms of capital. In J. G. Richardson (Ed.), *Handbook of theory and research for the sociology of education* (pp. 241–258). New York: Greenwood Press.

Bourdieu, P. (1990). The scholastic point of view. *Cultural Anthropology, 5*(4), 380–391.

Bourdieu, P., and Passeron, J. (1979). *The inheritors, French students and their relation to culture.* Chicago: University of Chicago Press.

Bourdieu, P., and Wacquant, L. (1992). *An invitation to reflexive sociology.* Chicago: University of Chicago Press.

Boureiko, N. (2010). *Factors influencing the academic success of second generation immigrant college students.* (Unpublished doctoral dissertation). University of Arkansas, Little Rock.

Brettell, C. B., and Nibbs, F. (2009). Lived hybridity: Second-generation identity construction through college festival. *Identities: Global Studies in Culture and Power, 16*(6), 678–699.

Brilliant, J. J. (2000). Issues in counseling immigrant college students. *Community College Journal of Research and Practice, 24*(7), 577–586.

Bronfenbrenner, U. (1979). *The ecology of human development.* Cambridge: Harvard University Press.

Bronfenbrenner, U. (1993). Ecology of cognitive development: Research models and fugitive findings. In R. H. Wozniak and K. W. Fischer (Eds.), *Development in context: Acting and thinking in specific environments* (pp. 3–44). Hillsdale, NJ: Erlbaum.

Bronfenbrenner, U., and Morris, P. A. (2006). The bioecological model of human development. In W. Damon and R. M. Lerner (Eds.), *Handbook of child psychology: Vol. 1. Theoretical models of human development* (6th ed., pp. 793–828). Hoboken, NJ: Wiley.

Brown, L. J. (2004). *The literature of immigration and racial reform: Becoming White, becoming other, becoming American in the late progressive era.* New York: Routledge.

Bruno, A. (2011). *Unauthorized alien students: Issues and "DREAM Act" legislation.* Washington, DC: Congressional Research Service.

Buddington, S. (2002). Acculturation, psychological adjustment (stress, depression, self-esteem) and the academic achievement of Jamaican immigrant college students. *International Social Work, 45*(4), 447–464.

Butcher, K. F., and Piehl, A. M. (2008). *Crime, corrections, and California: What does immigration have to do with it?* San Francisco: Public Policy Institute of California.

Cabrera, A. F., and La Nasa, S. M. (2000). *Understanding the college choice of disadvantaged students*. New Directions for Institutional Research, no. 107. San Francisco: Jossey-Bass.

Callahan, R. (2005). Tracking and high school English learners: Limiting opportunity to learn. *American Educational Research Journal, 42*(2), 305–328.

Callahan, R., Wilkinson, L., Muller, C., and Frisco, M. (2009). ESL placement and schools: Effects on immigrant achievement. *Educational Policy, 23*(2), 355–384.

Camarota, S. A. (2011). *A record-setting decade of immigration: 2000 to 2010*. Washington, DC: Center for Immigration Studies.

Camarota, S. A., and McArdle, N. (2003). *Where immigrants live: An examination of state residency of the foreign born by country of origin*. Washington, DC: Center for Immigration Studies.

Capps, R., and others. (2005). *The new demography of America's schools: Immigration and the No Child Left Behind Act*. Washington, DC: Urban Institute.

Carnevale, A. P., Smith, N., and Strohl, J. (2010). *Help wanted: Projection of jobs and education requirements through 2018*. Washington, DC: Georgetown University Center on Education and the Workforce.

Chapman, C., Laird, J., and KewalRamani, A. (2010). *Trends in high school dropout and completion rates in the United States: 1972–2008, compendium report*. Washington, DC: National Center for Education Statistics.

Chau, W. (2006). *The relationship between acculturative stress and spirituality among Chinese immigrant college students in the United States*. (Unpublished doctoral dissertation). California State University, Long Beach.

Chen, L., Gunderson, L., and Seror, J. (2005). Multiple perspectives on educationally resilient immigrant students. *TESL Canada Journal, 22*(2), 55–74.

Chickering, A. W., and Reisser, L. (1993). *Education and identity* (2nd ed.). San Francisco: Jossey-Bass.

Chin, A., and Juhn, C. (2007). *Does reducing college costs improve educational outcomes for undocumented immigrants?* Houston, TX: James A. Baker III Institute for Public Policy, Rice University.

Chirkov, V. (2009). Critical psychology of acculturation: What do we study and how do we study it, when we investigate acculturation? *International Journal of Intercultural Psychology, 33*(2), 94–105.

Chiswick, B. R. (1999). Are immigrants favorably self-selected? *American Economic Review, 89*(2), 181–185.

Chiswick, B. R., and DebBurman, N. (2004). Educational attainment: Analysis by immigrant generation. *Economics of Education Review, 23*(4), 361–379.

Cohen, A. M., and Brawer, F. B. (2003). *The American community college* (4th ed.). San Francisco: Jossey-Bass.

Coleman, J. S. (1988). Social capital in the creation of human capital. *American Journal of Sociology, 94*, 95–120.

The College Board. (2011). *Trends in college pricing, 2011*. New York: The College Board. Retrieved January 8, 2012, from http://trends.collegeboard.org/downloads/College_Pricing_2011.pdf.

Community College Consortiums for Immigrant Education. (2011). Promising practices. Retrieved January 14, 2012, from www.cccie.org/community-college-immigration-promising-practices.

Conway, K. M. (2009). Exploring persistence of immigrant and native students in an urban community college. *Review of Higher Education, 32*(3), 321–352.

Conway, K. M. (2010). Educational aspirations in an urban community college: Differences between immigrant and native student groups. *Community College Review, 37*(3), 209–242.

Cooper, C. R., and others. (2002). Bridging multiple worlds: How African American and Latino youth in academic outreach programs navigate math pathways to college. *Applied Developmental Science, 6*(2), 73–87.

Corey, A. T. (2000). *Correlates of Asian American college students' career aspirations: Generational status, self-reports, and parental-reports on acculturation and perceived prejudice.* (Unpublished doctoral dissertation). University of Nebraska, Lincoln.

Cortes, R. D. (2008). *Cursed and blessed: Examining the socioemotional and academic experiences of undocumented Latina/o community college students.* (Doctoral dissertation). Retrieved from ProQuest Dissertation and Thesis. (UMI 3318524)

Crandall, J., and Sheppard, K. (2004). *Adult ESL and the community college, working paper 7.* New York: Council for Advancement of Adult Literacy.

Crosby, C. R. (2010). Academic identities under construction: Academic literacies and identities of developmental immigrant students. *Research and Teaching in Developmental Education, 26*(2), 30–45.

Cuellar, I., Arnold, B., and Maldonado, R. (1995). Acculturation Rating Scale for Mexican Americans–II: A revision of the original ARSMA Scale. *Hispanic Journal of Behavioral Sciences, 17*(3), 275–304.

Damm, A. P. (2009). Ethnic enclaves and immigrant labour market outcomes: Quasi experimental evidence. *Journal of Labor Economics, 27*(2), 281–314.

Day v. Sebelius, 376 F.Supp.2d 1022 (2005).

De la Garza, R. O., Falcon, A., and Garcia, F. C. (1996). Will the real Americans please stand up: Anglo and Mexican-American support of core American political values. *American Journal of Political Science, 40*(2), 335–351.

De La Rosa, M. L. (2006). Is opportunity knocking? *American Behavioral Scientist, 49*(12), 1670–1686.

De Leon, S. A. (2005). *Assimilation and ambiguous experience of the resilient male Mexican immigrants that successfully navigate American higher education.* (Doctoral dissertation). Retrieved from ProQuest Digital Dissertations. (AAT 3174419)

DebBurman, N. (2005). *Immigrant education: Variations by generation, age-at-immigration, and country of origin.* New York: LFB Scholarly Publishing.

Desai, J. S. (2006). *Intergenerational conflict within Asian American families: The role of acculturation, ethnic identity, individualism, and collectivism.* (Unpublished doctoral dissertation). Loyola University, Chicago.

Dickson, L. M., and Pender, M. (2010). *Do in-state tuition benefits affect the enrollment of noncitizens? Evidence from universities in Texas.* Retrieved November 29, 2011, from www.umbc.edu/economics/wpapers/wp_10_125.pdf.

Dika, S. L., and Singh, K. (2002). Applications of social capital in educational literature: A critical synthesis. *Review of Educational Research, 72*(1), 31–60.

DiNapoli, T. P., and Bleiwas, K. B. (2010). *The role of immigrants in the New York economy* (Report 17-2010). New York: Office of State Comptroller.

Do, V. T. (1996). Counseling culturally different students in the community college. *Community College Journal of Research and Practice, 20*(1), 9–21.

Dougherty, K. J., Nienhusser, H. K., and Vega, B. E. (2010). Undocumented immigrants and state higher education policy: The politics of in-state tuition eligibility in Texas and Arizona. *Review of Higher Education, 34*(1), 123–173.

Dougherty, K., and Reid, M. (2007). *Fifty states of achieving the dream: State policies to enhance access to and success in community colleges across the United States.* New York: Teacher's College, Community College Research Center, Columbia University.

Douglass, J. A., and Thomson, G. (2010). The immigrant's university: A study of academic performance and the experiences of recent immigrant groups at the University of California. *Higher Education Policy, 23*(4), 451–474.

D'Souza, D. (1991). *Illiberal education.* New York: Vintage.

Ellis, P. A. (1995). Language minority students: Are community colleges meeting the challenge? *Community College Journal, 65*(6), 26–33.

Enriquez, L. E. (2011). Because we feel the pressure and we also feel the support: Examining the educational success of undocumented immigrant Latina/o students. *Harvard Educational Review, 81*(3), 476–500.

Erisman, W., and Looney, S. (2007). *Opening the door to the American dream: Increasing higher education and success for immigrants.* Washington, DC: Institute for Higher Education Policy.

Evans, N. J., and others. (2010). *Student development in college: Theory, research, and practice* (2nd ed.). San Francisco: Jossey-Bass.

Faltis, C., and Coulter, C. (2008). *Teaching English learners and immigrant students in secondary schools.* Boston: Pearson-Merrill Prentice.

Feliciano, C. (2006). *Unequal origins: Immigrant selection and the education of the second generation.* New York: LFB Scholarly Publishing.

Fix, M., and Passel, J. S. (2003). *U.S. immigration: Trends and implications for schools.* Washington, DC: Urban Institute.

Flores, S. M. (2010). State dream acts: The effect of in-state resident tuition policies and undocumented Latino students. *Review of Higher Education, 33*(2), 239–283.

Flores, S. M., and Chapa, J. (2009). Latino immigrant access to higher education in a bipolar context of reception. *Journal of Hispanic Higher Education, 8*(1), 90–109.

Flores, S. M., and Horn, C. L. (2009). College persistence among undocumented students at a selective public university: A quantitative case study analysis. *Journal of College Student Retention: Research, Theory & Practice, 11*(1), 57–76.

Fraga, L. R., and Segura, G. M. (2006). Culture clash? Contesting notions of American identity and the effects of Latin American immigration. *Perspectives on Politics, 4*(2), 279–287.

Frey, W. H. (1995). Immigration and internal migration flight: A California case study. *Population and Environment, 16*(4), 353–375.

Frey, W. H. (1996). Immigration, domestic migration, and demographic balkanization in America: New Evidence for the 1990s. *Population and Development Review, 22*(4), 741–763.

Frum, J. L. (2007). Postsecondary educational access for undocumented students: Opportunities and constraints. *American Academic, 3,* 81–107.

Fry, R. (2002). *Latinos in higher education: Many enroll, too few graduate.* Washington, DC: Pew Hispanic Center.

Fry, R. (2003). *Hispanic youth dropping out of U.S. schools: Measuring the challenge.* Washington, DC: Pew Hispanic Center.

Fukuyama, F. (1993). Immigrants and family values. *Commentary, 95*(5), 26–32.

Fuligni, A. J., and Pedersen, S. (2002). Family obligation and the transition to young adulthood. *Developmental Psychology, 38*(5), 856–868.

Fuligni, A. J., Tseng, V., and Lam, M. (1999). Attitudes toward family obligations among American adolescents from Asian, Latin American, and European backgrounds. *Child Development, 70,* 1030–1044.

Fuligni, A. J., and Witkow, M. (2004). The postsecondary educational progress of youth from immigrant families. *Journal of Research on Adolescence, 14*(2), 159–183.

Gándara, P. (2007, April). *NCLB and California English language learners.* Paper presented at the annual meeting of the American Education Research Association, Chicago.

Gándara, P., and Contreras, F. (2009). *The Latino education crisis: The consequences of failed policies.* Cambridge, MA: Harvard University Press.

Garcia, G. E. (2000). Bilingual children's reading. In M. L. Kamil, P. B. Mosenthal, P. D. Pearson, and R. Barr (Eds.), *Handbook of reading research* (Vol. 3, pp. 813–834). Mahwah, NJ: Erlbaum.

Garcia, O., Kleifgen, J. A., and Falchi, L. (2008). *From English language learners to emergent bilinguals: Equity matters. Research Review No. 1. Equity in education forum series.* New York: Teachers College, Columbia University.

Garcia Coll, C., and Magnusson, K. (1997). The psychological experience of immigration: A developmental perspective. In A. Booth, A. C. Crouter, and N. Landale (Eds.), *Immigration and the family: Research and policy on U.S. immigrants* (pp. 91–132). Mahwah, NJ: Erlbaum.

Gergen, K. J. (1991). *The saturated self: Dilemmas of identity in contemporary life.* New York: Basic Books.

Gibson, M. A. (1997). Complicating the immigrant/involuntary minority typology. *Anthropology & Education Quarterly, 28*(3), 431–454.

Gibson, M. A., and Ogbu, J. U. (1991). *Minority status and schooling: A comparative study of immigrant vs. involuntary minorities.* New York: Garland.

Goldschmidt, M. M., and Ousey, D. L. (2011). *Teaching developmental immigrant students in undergraduate programs.* Lansing: University of Michigan Press.

Gonzalez, A., and De La Torre, A. (2002). The educational outcomes of Hispanics and non-Hispanics in Arizona: Implications for national and state policy makers. *Educational Policy, 16*(2), 288–310.

Gonzales, R. G. (2007). Wasted talent and broken dreams: The lost potential of undocumented Students. *Immigration Policy in Focus, 5*(13), 1–11.

Gonzales, R. G. (2009). *Young lives on hold: The college dreams of undocumented students.* Washington, DC: College Board.

Gordon, M. M. (1964). *Assimilation in American life.* New York: Oxford University Press.

Goyette, K., and Xie, Y. (1999). Educational expectations of Asian American youths: Determinants and ethnic differences. *Sociology of Education, 72*(1), 22–36.

Gray, M. J., Rolph, E. S., and Melamid, E. (1996). Immigration and higher education: Institutional responses to changing demographics. Santa Monica, CA: RAND.

Grieco, E. M. (2006). *Temporary admission of nonimmigrants to the United States: 2005.* Washington, DC: Office of Immigration Statistics, Policy Directorate, U.S. Department of Homeland Security.

Gryn, T. A., and Larsen, L. J. (2010). *Nativity status and citizenship in the United States: 2009* (ACSBR/09-16). Washington, DC: U.S. Census Bureau.

Hagy, A. P., and Staniec, J.F.O. (2002). Immigrant status, race, and institutional choice in higher education. *Economics of Education Review, 21*(4), 381–392.

Hao, L., and Bonstead-Bruns, M. (1998). Parent-child differences in educational expectations and the academic achievement of immigrant and native students. *Sociology of Education, 71*(3), 175–198.

Harklau, L. (1994). Jumping tracks: How language-minority students negotiate evaluations of ability. *Anthropology and Education Quarterly, 25*(3), 347–363.

Harklau, L. (1998). Newcomers in U.S. higher education: Issues of access and equity. *Educational Policy, 12*(6), 634–658.

Harklau, L., Losey, K. M., and Siegal, M. (1999). *Generation 1.5 meets college composition: Issues in the teaching of writing to U.S.-educated learners of ESL.* Mahwah, NJ: Erlbaum.

Haskins, R. (2007). *Immigration: Wages, education and mobility. Economic Mobility Project.* Washington, DC: Brookings Institution.

Heilig, J. V., Rodriguez, C., and Somers, P. (2011). Immigrant DREAMs: English learners, the Texas 10% admissions plan, and college academic success. *Journal of Latinos and Education, 10*(2), 106–126.

Hoefer, M., Rytina, N., and Baker, B. (2010). *Estimates of the unauthorized immigrant population residing in the United States: January 2009.* Washington, DC: Office of Immigrant Statistics.

Hoerder, D., Hebert, Y., and Schmitt, I. (Eds.) (2006). *Negotiating transcultural lives: Belongings and social capital among youth in comparative perspective.* Toronto, Ontario: University of Toronto Press.

Hoover-Dempsey, K. V., and Sandler, H. M. (1997). Why do parents become involved in their children's education? *Review of Educational Research, 67*(1), 3–42.

Horvat, E. M. (2001). Understanding equity and access in higher education: The potential contribution of Pierre Bourdieu. In J. C. Smart (Ed.), *Higher education: Handbook of the theory and practice* (Vol. 16, pp. 195–238). New York: Agathon.

Hossler, D., Schmit, J., and Vesper, N. (1999). *Going to college: How social, economic, and educational factors influence the decisions students make.* Baltimore: Johns Hopkins University Press.

Huang, C. M. (2006). *Acculturation, Asian cultural values, family conflict, and perceived stress in Chinese immigrant female college students in the United States.* (Unpublished doctoral dissertation). Alliant International University, Los Angeles.

Huang, K. Y. (2007). Reimaging and redefining the DREAM: A proposal for improving access to higher education for undocumented immigrants. *Seattle Journal for Social Justice, 6,* 431–456.

Huber, L. (2009). Challenging racist nativist framing: Acknowledging the community cultural wealth of undocumented Chicana college students to reframe the immigration debate. *Harvard Educational Review, 79*(4), 704–729.

Hudson, R., Towey, J., and Shinar, O. (2008). Depression and racial/ethnic variations within a diverse nontraditional college sample. *College Student Journal, 42*(1), 103–114.

Hunt, J. B., and Tierney, T. J. (2006). *American higher education: How does it measure up for the 21st Century.* San Jose, CA: National Center for Public Policy and Higher Education.

Hurtado, S., and Carter, D. F. (1997). Effects of college transition and perceptions of the campus racial climate on Latino college students' sense of belonging. *Sociology of Education, 70*(4), 324–345.

Inman, A. G., Howard, E. E., Beaumont, R. L., and Walker, J. A. (2007). Cultural transmission: Influence of contextual factors in Asian Indian immigrant parents' experiences. *Journal of Counseling Psychology, 54*(1), 93–100.

Jaret, C., and Reitzes, D. C. (2009). Currents in a stream: College student identities and ethnic identities and their relationship with self-esteem, efficacy, and grade point average in an urban university. *Social Science Quarterly, 90*(2), 345–367.

Jauregui, J. A. (2007). *Analysis of factors impacting Texas borderland community colleges' role in educating undocumented students*. (Doctoral dissertation). Retrieved from ProQuest. (UMI 3274039).

Jefferys, K., and Rytina, N. (2006). *U.S. legal permanent residents: 2005*. Washington, DC: Office of Immigration Statistics, U.S. Department of Homeland Security.

Jenkins, A. H., Harburg, E., Weissberg, N. C., and Donnelly, T. (2004). The influence of minority group cultured models on persistence in college. *Journal of Negro Education, 73*(1), 69–80.

Jensen, L. (2001). The demographic diversity of immigrants and their children. In R. G. Rumbaut and A. Portes (Eds.), *Ethnicities: Children of immigrants in America* (pp. 21–56). Berkeley: The Russell Sage Foundation and University of California Press.

Jiménez, T. R. (2011). *Immigrants in the United States: How well are they integrating into society?* Washington, DC: Migration Policy Institute.

Jung, M-K. (2009). The racial unconscious of assimilation theory. *DuBois Review, 6*(2), 375–395.

Kao, G. (2004). Social capital and its relevance to minority and immigrant population. *Sociology of Education, 77*(2), 172–175.

Kao, G., and Thompson, J. (2003). Race and ethnic stratification in educational achievement and attainment. *Annual Review of Sociology, 29*(1), 417–442.

Kao, G., and Tienda, M. (1995). Optimism and achievement: The educational performance of immigrant youth. *Social Science Quarterly, 76*(1), 1–19.

Kao, G., and Tienda, M. (1998). Educational aspirations of minority youth. *American Journal of Education,* 106, 349–384.

Kasinitz, P., Mollenkopf, J. H., Waters, M. C., and Holdaway, J. (2008). *Inheriting the city: The children of immigrants come of age.* Cambridge, MA: Harvard University Press.

Kaushal, N. (2008). In-state tuition for the undocumented: Education effects on Mexican adults. *Journal of Policy Analysis and Management, 27*(4), 771–792.

Keller, U., and Tillman, K. (2008). Post-secondary educational attainment of immigrant and native youth. *Social Forces, 87*(1), 121–152.

Kim, B.S.K., and Abreu, J. M. (2001). Acculturation measurement: Theory, current instruments, and future directions. In J. G. Ponterotto, J. M. Casas, L. A. Suzuki, and C. M. Alexander (Eds.), *Handbook of multicultural counseling* (2nd ed., pp. 394–424). Thousand Oaks, CA: Sage.

Kim, D. H., and Schneider, B. (2005). Social capital in action: Alignment of parental support in adolescents' transition to postsecondary education. *Social Forces, 84*(2), 1181–1206.

Kim, E. (2008). Korean American adolescent depression and parenting. *Journal of Child and Adolescent Psychiatric Nursing, 21*(2), 105–115.

Kim, E. (2009). Navigating college life: The role of peer networks in first-year college adaptation experience of minority immigrant students. *Journal of the First-Year Experience & Students in Transition, 21*(2), 9–34.

Kim, E. (2010, April). *Racial and ethnic identities of minority immigrant college students*. Paper presented at the annual meeting of the American Educational Research Association, New Orleans, LA.

Kim, E., and Kamnoetsin, T. (2011, November). *Parents' college expectations and involvement: The role of social class and ethnicity in generation 1.5 Chinese and Korean immigrants*. Paper presented at the annual meeting of Association for the Study of Higher Education, Charlotte, NC.

Kim, R. (2004). Second-generation Korean American evangelicals: Ethnic, multiethnic, or white campus ministries? *Sociology of Religion, 65*(1), 19–34.

Kindler, A. (2002). *Survey of the state's limited English proficiency of students and available education programs and services: 2000–2001*. Washington, DC: U.S. Department of Education.

King, J. E. (2004). *Missed opportunities: Students who do not apply for financial aid*. Washington, DC: American Council on Education Issue Brief.

Klein, S., Bugarin, R., Beltranena, R., and McArthur, E. (2004). *Language minorities and their educational and labor market indicators: Recent trends*. NCES 2004-009. Washington, D.C.: National Center for Education Statistics, U.S. Department of Education.

Kobach, K. W. (2007). Immigration nullification: In-state tuition and lawmakers who disregard the law. *NYUJ Legislation and Public Policy, 10*, 473–523.

Kuo, E. W. (1999). English as a second language in the community college curriculum. In A. C. Bueschel and A. Venezia (Ed.), *Policies and practices to improve student preparation and success* (pp. 69–80). New Directions for Community Colleges, Vol. 108. San Francisco: Jossey-Bass.

Lamont, M., and Lareau, A. (1988). Cultural capital: Allusions, gaps and glissandos in recent theoretical developments. *Sociological Theory, 6*(2), 153–68.

Lareau, A. (1987). Social class differences in family-school relationships: The importance of cultural capital. *Sociology of Education, 60*(2), 73–85.

Lareau, A. (2001). Linking Bourdieu's concept of capital to the broader field: The case of family-school relationships. In B. J. Biddle (Ed.), *Social class, poverty, and education: Policy and practice* (pp. 77–100). New York: Routlege/Falmer.

Lee, J. J., and Rice, C. (2007). Welcome to America? International student perceptions of discrimination. *Higher Education, 53*(3), 381–409.

Lee, J. S., and Suarez, D. (2009). A synthesis of the roles of heritage languages in the lives of immigrant children. In T. Wiley, J. S. Lee, and R. Rumberger (Eds.), *The education of language minority students in the United States* (pp. 136–171). Clevedon, UK: Multilingual Matters.

Lee, R. M., and Andrea B. Y. (2010). Comparing the ethnic identity and well-being of adopted Korean Americans with immigrant/U.S.-born Korean Americans and Korean international students. *Adoption Quarterly, 13*(1), 2–17.

Lee, S. J. (1994). Behind the model-minority stereotype: Voices of high- and low-achieving Asian American students. *Anthropology & Education Quarterly, 25*(4), 413–429.

Lee, V. E., and Ekstrom, R. B. (1987). Student access to guidance counseling in high school. *American Educational Research Journal, 24*(2), 287–310.

Leong, F.T.L., and Gim-Chung, R. H. (1995). Career assessment and intervention with Asian Americans. In F.T.L. Leong (Ed.), *Career development and vocational behavior of ethnic and racial minorities* (pp. 1–6). Mahwah, NJ: Erlbaum.

Lew, J. (2006). Asian Americans in class: *Charting the achievement gap among Korean American Youth*. New York: Teachers College Press.

Lew, J. W., Chang, J. C., and Wang, W. (2005). UCLA community college review: The overlooked minority: Asian Pacific American students at community colleges. *Community College Review, 33*(2), 64–84.

Lin, N. (1999a). Building a network theory of social capital. *Connections, 22*(1), 28–51.

Lin, N. (1999b). Social networks and status attainment. *Annual Review of Sociology, 25*(1), 467–487.

Lin, N. (2001). *Social capital: A theory of social structure and action.* Cambridge, MA: Cambridge University Press.

Lipman, F. J. (2006). Taxing undocumented immigrants: Separate, unequal, and without representation. *Tax Lawyer, 59*(3), 813–866.

Liu, J. M., Ong, P. M., and Rosenstein, C. (1991). Dual chain migration: Post-1965 Filipino immigration to the United States. *International Migration Review, 25*(3), 487–513.

Long, B. T., and Riley, E. (2007). Financial aid: A broken bridge to college access? *Harvard Educational Review, 77*(1), 39–63.

Lopez, J. K. (2006). The impact of demographic changes on U.S. higher education: 2000–2050. Boulder, CO: State Higher Education Executive Officers.

Lopez, M. P. (2005). Reflections on educating Latino and Latina undocumented children: Beyond *Plyler v. Doe. Seton Hall Law Review, 35*, 1373–1406.

Lopez, N. (2003). *Hopeful girls and troubled boys: Race and gender disparity in urban education.* New York: Routledge.

Louie, V. S. (2001). Parents' aspirations and investment: The role of social class in the educational experiences of 1.5-and second-generation Chinese Americans. *Harvard Educational Review, 71*(3), 438–474.

Louie, V. S. (2004). *Compelled to excel: Immigration, education, and opportunity among Chinese Americans.* CA: Stanford University Press.

Louie, V. S. (2005). Immigrant newcomer populations, ESEA, and the pipeline to college: Current considerations and future lines of inquiry. *Review of Research in Education, 29*, 69–105.

Lumina Foundation. (2009). *A stronger nation through higher education: How and why Americans must meet a big goal for college attainment.* Indianapolis, IN: Lumina Foundation.

Maramba, D. C. (2008). Immigrant families and the college experience: Perspectives of Filipina Americans. *Journal of College Student Development, 49*(4), 336–350.

Martin, D. C. (2011, March). *Annual report: Refugees and asylees: 2010.* Washington, DC: Office of Immigration Statistics, U.S. Department of Homeland Security.

Martin, P., and Midgley, E. (2010). *Population bulletin update: Immigration in America 2010.* Washington, DC: Population Reference Bureau.

Martinez v. Regents of the University of California, 50 CAL 4th 1277 (2010).

Massey, D. S. (1987). Understanding Mexican migration to the United States. *American Journal of Sociology, 92*(6), 1372–1403.

Massey, D. S., Alarcon, R., Durand, J., and Gonzalez, H. (1987). *Return to Azatlan: The social process of international migration from Western Mexico.* Berkeley: University of California.

Massey, D. S., Durand, J., and Malone, N. J. (2002). *Beyond smoking mirrors: Mexican immigration in an era of economic integration.* New York: Russell Sage Foundation.

Mau, W. C. (1995). Educational planning and academic achievement of middle school students: A racial/cultural comparison. *Journal of Counseling and Development, 73*(5), 518–526.

Mau, W. C. (1997). Parental influences on the high school students' academic achievement: A comparison of Asian, Asian Americans, and White Americans. *Psychology in the Schools, 34*(3), 267–277.

McDonough, P. M. (1997). *Choosing colleges: How social class and schools structure opportunity.* New York: State University of New York Press.

McDonough, P. M., and Calderone, S. (2004). The meaning of money: Perceptual differences between college counselors and low-income families about college costs and financial aid. *American Behavioral Scientist, 49*(12), 1703–1718.

McDonough, P. M., Ventresca, M. V., and Outcalt, C. L. (2000). Field of dreams: Understanding sociohistorical changes in college access, 1965–1995. In J. C. Smart, and W. G. Tierney (Eds.), *Higher education: Handbook of theory and research* (Vol. 15, pp. 371–405). New York: Agathon Press.

McEwen, M. K. (2003). The nature and uses of theory. In S. R. Komives and D. B. Woodard, Jr. (Eds.), *Student services: A handbook for the profession* (4th ed., pp. 153–178). San Francisco: Jossey-Bass.

Menjívar, C. (2000). *Fragmented ties: Salvadoran immigrant networks in America.* Berkeley: University of California Press.

Montreuil, A., and Bourhis, R. Y. (2001). Majority acculturation orientations toward valued and devalued immigrants. *Journal of Cross-Cultural Psychology, 32*(6), 698–719.

Muñoz, S. M. (2008). *Understanding issues of college persistence for undocumented Mexican immigrant women from the new Latino diaspora: A case study.* (Doctoral dissertation). Retrieved from ProQuest Dissertation and Theses. (UMI 3316177)

Museus, S. D., and Maramba, D. C. (2011). The impact of culture on Filipino American students' sense of belonging. *Review of Higher Education, 34*(2), 231–258.

Nadadur, R. (2009). Illegal immigration: A positive economic contribution to the United States. *Journal of Ethnic and Migration Studies, 35*(6), 1037–1052.

National Conference of State Legislatures. (2011, June). Enacted immigrant related laws and resolutions: January-June 2011. Retrieved from www.ncsl.org/portals/1/documents/immig/Enacted_Immigrant_LawsJune2011pdf.

National Immigration Law Center. (2006, April). *Basic facts about in-state tuition for undocumented immigrant students.* Retrieved November 28, 2011, from www.nilc.org/immlawpolicy/DREAM/in-state_tuition_basicfacts_041706.pdf.

National Immigration Law Center. (2011, October). *State bills on access to education for immigrants: Tuition equity bills.* Retrieved December 15, 2011, from www.nilc.org/improveaccesstuition.html.

Nazon, M. C. (2010). *A study of predictors of college completion among SEEK immigrant Students.* (Doctoral dissertation). Retrieved from ProQuest Dissertation and Theses. (UMI 3396451).

Neisser, U. (1986). New answers to an old question. In U. Neisser (Ed.), *The school achievement of minority children* (pp. 1–18). Hillsdale, NJ: Erlbaum.

Ngo, B., and Lee, S. (2007). Complicating the image of model minority success: A review of Southeast Asian American education. *Review of Educational Research, 77*(4), 415–453.

Noguera, P. A. (2004). Social capital and education of immigrant students: Categories and generalizations. *Sociology of Education, 77*(2), 180–183.

Nuñez, A. M. (2004). Using segmented assimilation theory to enhance conceptualization of college participation. *InterActions: UCLA Journal of Education and Information Studies, 1*(1), 1–21.

Nuñez, A-M., and Sparks, P. J. (2012). Who are linguistic minority students in higher education?: An analysis of the Beginning Postsecondary Students Study 2004. In Y. Kanno and L. Harklau (Eds.), *Linguistic minority students go to college: Preparation, access, and persistence* (pp. 110–129). New York: Routledge.

Ogbu, J. (1990). Minority education in comparative perspective. *Journal of Negro Education,* 59(1), 45–57.

Oh, S. S., and Cooc, N. (2011). Immigration, youth, and education: Editors' introduction. *Harvard Educational Review, 81*(3), 397–407.

Olivas, M. A. (2004). IIRIRA, the DREAM act and undocumented college students' residency. *Journal of Colleges and Universities, 30,* 435–464.

Oliverez, P. M. (2005, April). *College-ready but undocumented: The challenges of college access for undocumented students in the U.S.* Paper presented at the annual meeting of the American Educational Research Association, Montreal, Canada.

Oliverez, P. M. (2006). *Ready but restricted: An examination of the challenges of colleges-ready undocumented students in the United States.* (Doctoral dissertation). Retrieved from ProQuest. (AAT 3257819)

Oliverez, P. M., Chavez, M. L., Soriano, M., and Tierney, W. G. (2006). *The college and financial aid guide for AB 540 undocumented immigrant students.* Los Angeles: University of Southern California, Center for Higher Education Policy Analysis.

Ordovensky, J. F., and Hagy, A. P. (1998). *Immigrant status, race, and institutional choice in higher education.* Washington, DC: Center for Economic Studies.

Orozco, G. L. (2008). Understanding the culture of low-income immigrant Latino parents: Key to involvement. *The School Community Journal, 18*(1), 21–37.

Ortiz, A. M., and Santos, S. J. (2009). *Ethnicity in college: Advancing theory and diversity practices on campus.* Arlington, VA: Stylus.

Passel, J. S. (1999). Undocumented immigration to the United States: Numbers, trends and characteristics. In D. W. Haines and K. E. Rosenblum (Eds.), *Illegal immigration in America* (pp. 27–111). Westport, CT: Greenwood Press.

Passel, J. S. (2003). *Further demographic information relating to the DREAM Act.* Washington, DC: Urban Institute.

Passel, J. S., and Cohn, D. (2008). *Trends in unauthorized immigration: Undocumented inflow now trails legal inflow.* Washington, DC: Pew Hispanic Center.

Passel, J. S., and Cohn, D. (2011). *Unauthorized immigrant population: National and state trends, 2010.* Washington, DC: Pew Hispanic Center.

Passel, J. S., and Cohn, D. (2012). *U.S. foreign-born population: How much change from 2009 to 2010?* Washington, DC: Pew Hispanic Center.

Passel, J. S., and Lopez, M. H. (2012). Up to 1.7 million unauthorized immigrant youth may benefit from new deportation rules. Washington, DC: Pew Hispanic Center. Retrieved July 1, 2012, from www.pewhispanic.org/files/2012/08/PewHispanic-unauthorized-immigrant-youth-new-deportation-policy.pdf.

Patten, E. (2012). *Statistical portrait of the foreign-born population in the United States, 2010.* Washington, DC: Pew Hispanic Center.

Perez, P. (2010). College choice process of Latino undocumented students: Implications for recruitment and retention. *Journal of College Admissions,* 206, 21–25.

Perez, W. (2009). *We are Americans: Undocumented students pursuing the American dream.* Alexandria, VA: Sterling.

Perez, W., and others. (2009). Academic resilience among undocumented Latino students. *Hispanic Journal of Behavioral Science, 21*(2), 149–181.

Perez Huber, L., and Malagon, M. (2007). Silenced struggles: The experiences of Latina and Latino undocumented college students in California. *Nevada Law Journal, 7*(3), 841–861.

Perez Huber, L., and others. (2006). *Falling through the cracks: Critical transition in the Latino educational pipeline: 2006 educational summit report.* Los Angeles: UCLA Chicano Studies Research Center.

Perna, L. W. (2000). Difference in the decision to attend college among African Americans, Hispanics and Whites. *Journal of Higher Education, 71*(2), 117–141.

Perna, L. W. (2004). Impact of student aid program design, operations, and marketing on the formation of family college-going plans and resulting college-going behaviors of potential students. Boston: Education Resources Institute (TERI).

Perna, L. W., and Titus, M. A. (2005). The relationship between parental involvement as social capital and college enrollment: An examination of racial/ethnic group differences. *Journal of Higher Education, 76*(5), 485–518.

Perreira, K. M., Harris, K. M., and Lee, D. (2006). Making it in America: High school completion by immigrant and native youth. *Demography, 43*(3), 511–536.

Perry, A. M. (2006). Toward a theoretical framework for membership: The case of undocumented immigrants and financial aid for postsecondary education. *Review of Higher Education, 30*(1), 21–40.

Pew Hispanic Center (2011). *Pew Hispanic Center tabulations of 2010 American Community Survey* (1% IPUMS).

Phinney, J. S. (1990). Ethnic identity in adolescents and adults: Review of research. *Psychological Bulletin, 108*(3), 499–514.

Phinney, J. S. (1992). The multigroup ethnic identity measure: A new scale for use with diverse groups. *Journal of Adolescent Research, 7*(2), 156–176.

Phinney, J. S. (1996). When we talk about American ethnic groups, what do we mean? *American Psychologist, 51*(9), 918–927.

Phinney, J. S. (2001). *The multigroup ethnic identity measure (MEIM).* Retrieved October 11, 2011, from www.calstatela.edu/academic/psych/ftp/meim.doc.

Phinney, J. S., Romero, I., Nava, M., and Huang, D. (2001). The role of language, parents, and peers in ethnic identity among adolescents in immigrant families. *Journal of Youth and Adolescence, 30*(2), 135–153.

Pizarro, M., and Vera, E. M. (2001). Chicana/o ethnic identity research: Lessons for researchers and counselors. *Counseling Psychologist, 29*(1), 91–117.

Poch, S. (2005). Higher education in a box. *International Journal of Educational Management, 19*(3), 246–258.

Pope, R. L. (2000). The relationship between psychosocial development and racial identity of college students of color. *Journal of College Student Development, 41*(3), 304–314.

Portes, A. (1997). Immigration theory for a new century: Some problems and opportunities. *The International Migration Review, 31*(4), 799–825.

Portes, A. (1998). Social capital: Its origins and applications in modern sociology. *Annual Review of Sociology, 24*(1), 1–24.

Portes, A. (2000). The two meanings of social capital. *Sociological Forum, 15*(1), 1–12.

Portes, A., Haller, W. J., and Guarnizo, L. (2002). Transnational entrepreneurs: An alternative form of immigrant economic adaptation. *American Sociological Review, 67*(2), 278–298.

Portes, A., and MacLeod, D. (1996). Educational progress of children of immigrants: The roles of class, ethnicity, and school context. *Sociology of Education, 69*(4), 255–275.

Portes, A., and Rumbaut, R. G. (1996). *Immigrant America: A portrait* (2nd ed.). Los Angeles: University of California Press.

Portes, A., and Rumbaut, R. G. (2001). *Legacies: The story of the immigrant second generation.* Los Angeles: University of California Press.

Portes, A., and Sensenbrenner, J. (1993). Embeddedness and immigration: Notes on the social determinants of economic action. *The American Journal of Sociology, 98*(6), 1320–1350.

Portes, A., and Zhou, M. (1993). The new second generation: Segmented assimilation and its variants. *Annals of the American Academy of Political and Social Science, 530*(1), 74–96.

Ream, R. K. (2001). *On the move: The mobility/social capital dynamic in the achievement gap between Mexican-American and non-Latino White adolescents.* (Doctoral dissertation). Retrieved from ProQuest Dissertations and Theses. (3024437).

Rector, R. (2006). *Senate immigration bill would allow 100 million new legal immigrants over the next twenty years.* (Web memo). Washington, DC: Heritage Foundation.

Renn, K. A., and Arnold, K. D. (2003). Reconceptualizing research on peer culture. *Journal of Higher Education, 74*(3), 261–291.

Rendón, L. I., Jalomo, R. E., and Nora, A. (2000). Theoretical considerations in the study of minority student retention in higher education. In J. M. Braxton (Ed.), *Reworking the student departure puzzle* (pp. 127–156). Nashville, TN: Vanderbilt University Press.

Rincon, A. (2008). *Undocumented immigrants and higher education. Sí se puede!* New York: LFB Scholarly.

Rivas, M. A., Pérez, J., Alvarez, C. R., and Solórzano, D. G. (2007). *An examination of Latina/o transfer students in California's postsecondary institutions* (No. 16). Los Angeles: UCLA Chicano Studies Research Center.

Robinson-Wood, T. (2009). Love, school, and money: Stress and cultural coping among ethnically diverse Black college women: A mixed-method analysis. *Western Journal of Black Studies, 33*(2), 77–86.

Rocha-Tracy, M. N. (2009). Encounters between immigrant students and U.S. urban universities. *Human Architecture: Journal of the Sociology of Self-Knowledge, 2*(1), 23–34.

Rodriguez, G. M., and Cruz, L. (2009). The transition to college of English learner and undocumented immigrant students: Resource and policy implications. *Teachers College Record, 111*(10), 1119–1152.

Romero, V. C. (2001). Postsecondary school education benefits for undocumented immigrants: Promises and pitfalls. *North Carolina Journal of International Law and Commercial Regulation, 27,* 393–418.

Rong, X. L., and Brown, F. (2001). The effects of immigrant generation and ethnicity on educational attainment among young African and Caribbean Blacks in the United States. *Harvard Educational Review, 71*(3), 536–565.

Rowan-Kenyon, H. T., Bell, A. D., and Perna, L. (2008). Contextual influences on parental involvement and college-going: Variations by socioeconomic class. *Journal of Higher Education, 79*(5), 564–586.

Roysircar, G., Carey, J., and Koroma, S (2010). Asian Indian college students math and science preferences: Influences of cultural contexts. *Journal of Career Development, 36*(4), 324–347.

Rudmin, F. (2009). Constructs, measurements and models of acculturation and acculturative stress. *International Journal of Intercultural Relations, 33*(2), 106–123.

Ruge, T. R., and Iza, A. D. (2004). Higher education for undocumented students: The case for open admission and in-state tuition rates for students without lawful immigration status. *Indiana International & Comparative Law Review, 15*(1), 257–278.

Ruge, T. R., and Iza, A. D. (2005). Higher education for undocumented students: The case for open admission and in-state tuition rates for students without lawful immigration status. *Indiana International and Comparative Law Review, 15*(2), 1–22.

Ruiz-de-Velasco, J., and Fix, M. (2000). *Overlooked and underserved: Immigrant students in U.S. secondary schools.* Washington, DC: Urban Institute Press.

Ruiz-de-Velasco, J., Fix, M., and Clewell, B. (2001). *Overlooked and underserved: Immigrant students in U.S. secondary schools.* Washington, DC: Urban Institute.

Rumbaut, R. G. (1994). The crucible within: Ethnic identity, self-esteem, and segmented assimilation among children of immigrants. *International Migration Review, 28*(4), 748–794.

Rumbaut, R. G. (2005). Turning points in the transition to adulthood: Determinants of educational attainment, incarceration, and early childbearing among children of immigrants. *Ethnic and Racial Studies, 28*(6), 1041–1086.

Rumbaut, R. G. (2007). Ages, life stages, and generational cohorts: Decomposing the immigrant first and second generations in the United States. In A. Portes and J. DeWind (Eds.), *Rethinking migration: New theoretical and empirical perspectives* (pp. 342–387). New York: Berghahn.

Rumbaut, R. G., and Ima, K. (1988). *The adaptation of Southeast Asian refugee youth: A comparative study.* Washington, DC: U.S. Office of Refugee Resettlement.

Rumbaut, R. G., and Portes, A. (Eds.) (2001). Ethnicities: Coming of age in immigrant America. Berkeley and New York: University of California Press and Russell Sage Foundation.

Russakoff, D. (2011). *Pre-K–3rd: Raising the educational performance of English language learners (ELLS).* Policy Action Brief, No. 6. Retrieved July 10, 2012, from http://fcdus.org/sites/default/files/FCD%20ELLsBrief6.pdf.

Russell, A. (2011, March). *Policy matters: State policies regarding undocumented college students: A narrative of unresolved issues, ongoing debate, and missed opportunities.* Retrieved May 18, 2011, from http://www.aascu.org/uploadedFiles/AASCU/Content/Root/PolicyAnd Advocacy/PolicyPublications/PM_UndocumentedStudents-March2011.pdf.

Ryder, A. G., Alden, L. E., and Paulhus, D. L. (2000). Is acculturation unidimensional or bidimensional? A head-to-head comparison in the prediction of personality, self-identity, and adjustment. *Journal of Personality and Social Psychology, 79*(1), 49–65.

Sallie Mae Fund. (2003). *Caught in the financial aid information divide.* Retrieved January 24, 2011, from www.thesalliemaefund.org/smfnew/pdf/TRPI_Key_Findings.pdf.

Schlesinger, A. (1992). *The disuniting of America.* New York: W. W. Norton.

Schneider, A. (2000). *Futures lost: Nostalgia and identity among Italian immigrants in Argentina.* Oxford: Peter Lang.

Schneider, B., and Lee, Y. (1990). A model for academic success: The school and home environment of East Asian students. *Anthropology and Education Quarterly, 21,* 358–377.

Schwartz, S. J., Unger, J. B., Zamboanga, B. L., and Szapocznik, J. (2010). Rethinking the concept of acculturation: Implications for theory and research. *American Psychologist, 65,* 237–251.

Schwartz, S. J., and others. (2011). Dimensions of acculturation: Associations with health risk behaviors among college students from immigrant families. *Journal of Counseling Psychology,* *58*(1), 27–41.

Seidman, R. H. (1995, April). *National education 'Goals 2000': Some disastrous unintended consequences.* Paper presented at the Annual Meeting of the American Educational Research Association, San Francisco, CA.

Sellers, R. M., and others. (1997). Multidimensional inventory of Black identity: Preliminary investigation of reliability and construct validity. *Journal of Personality and Social Psychology,* *73*(4), 805–815.

Serdarevic, M., and Chronister, K. (2005). Research with immigrant populations: The application of an ecological framework to mental health research with immigrant populations. *International Journal of Mental Health Promotion, 7*(2), 24–35.

Short, D. J., and Boyson, B. A. (2012). *Helping newcomer students succeed in secondary schools and beyond: A report to the Carnegie Corporation of New York.* Washington, DC: Center for Applied Linguistics.

Simanski, J., and Rytina, N. (2006, May). *Annual flow report: Naturalizations in the United States: 2005.* Washington, DC: Office of Immigration Statistics, U.S. Department of Homeland Security.

Skinner, C., and others. (2010). *English language proficiency, family economic security, and child development.* New York: Mailman School of Public Health, National Center for Children in Poverty, Columbia University.

Sluzki, C. (1979). Migration and family conflict. *Family Process, 18*(4), 379–390.

Smith, E. J. (1991). Ethnic identity development: Toward the development of a theory within the context of majority/minority status. *Journal of Counseling & Development, 70*(1), 181–188.

Sodowsky, G. R. (1991). Effects of culturally consistent counseling tasks on American and international student observers' perception of counselor credibility: A preliminary investigation. *Journal of Counseling & Development, 69*(3), 253–256.

Sodowsky, G. R., Kwan, K.L.K., and Pannu, R. (1995). Ethnic identity of Asians in the United States. In J. G. Ponterotto, J. M. Casas, L. A. Suzuki, and C. M. Alexander (Eds.), *Handbook of multicultural counseling* (pp. 123–154). Thousand Oaks, CA: Sage.

Soerens, M., and Hwang, J. (2009). *Welcoming the stranger: Justice, compassion, and the truth in the immigration debate.* Downers Grove, IL: InterVarsity Press.

Solórzano, D., and Villalpando, O. (1998). Critical race theory, marginality, and the experience of minority students in higher education. In C. Torres and T. Mitchell (Eds.), *Emerging issues in the sociology of education: Comparative perspectives* (pp. 211–224). Albany: State University of New York Press.

Solórzano, D. G., Rivas, M. A., and Velez, V. N. (2005, June). *Community college as a pathway to Chicana/o doctorate production* (Latino Policy Issues Brief No. 11). Los Angeles: Chicano Studies Research Center, University of California, Los Angeles.

Solórzano, D. G., Villalpando, O., and Oseguera, L. (2005). Educational inequities and Latina/o undergraduate students in the United States: A critical race analysis of their educational progress. *Journal of Hispanic Higher Education, 4*(3), 272–294.

Spears, A. K. (1999). Race and ideology: An introduction. In A. K. Spears (ed.), *Race and ideology: Language, symbolism, and popular culture* (pp. 11–58). Detroit: Wayne State University Press.

Stanton-Salazar, R. D. (2001). *Manufacturing hope and despair: The school and kin support networks of U.S. Mexican youth*. New York: Teachers College Press.

Stanton-Salazar, R. D. (2011). A social capital framework for the study of institutional agents and their role in the empowerment of low-status students and youth. *Youth & Society, 43*(3), 1066–1109.

Stanton-Salazar, R. D., and Dornbusch, S. M. (1995). Social capital and the reproduction of inequality: Information networks among Mexican-origin high school students. *Sociology of Education, 68*(2), 116–135.

Stanton-Salazar, R. D., and Spina, S. U. (2003). Informal mentors and role models in the lives of urban Mexican-origin adolescents. *Anthropology & Education Quarterly, 34*(3), 231–254.

Stebleton, M. J. (2007). Career counseling with African immigrant college students: Theoretical approaches and implications for practice. *Career Development Quarterly, 55*(4), 290–312.

Stebleton, M. J. (2010). The meaning of work for Black African immigrant adult college students. *Journal of Career Development, 39*(1), 50–75.

Stebleton, M. J., Huseman, R. L., and Kuzhabekova, A. (2010). *Do I belong here? Exploring immigrant college student responses on the SERU survey sense of belonging/satisfaction factor*. Research & Occasional Paper Series (CSHE 13.10). Berkeley: Center for Studies in Higher Education, University of California.

Stepick, A. (1996). Pride, prejudice and poverty: Economic, social, political and cultural capital among Haitians in Miami. In H. O. Duleep and P. V. Wunnava. (Eds.), *Immigrants and immigration policy: Individual skills, family ties, and group identities* (pp. 133–146). Greenwich, CT: JAI Press.

Suárez-Orozco, C. (2001). Psychocultural factors in the adaptation of immigrant youth: Gendered responses. In M. Agosín (Ed.), *Women and human rights: A global perspective* (pp. 170–188). Piscataway, NJ: Rutgers University Press.

Suarez-Orozco, C., and Suárez-Orozco, M. M. (1995). *Transformations: Immigration, family life, and achievement motivation among Latino adolescents*. Stanford, CA: Stanford University Press.

Suárez-Orozco, C., and Suárez-Orozco, M. M. (2001). *Children of immigration*. Cambridge, MA: Harvard University Press.

Suárez-Orozco, C., and Suárez-Orozco, M. M. (2009). Educating Latino immigrant students in the 21st century: Principles for the Obama administration. *Harvard Educational Review, 79*(2), 327–340.

Suárez-Orozco, C., Suárez-Orozco, M. M., and Todorova, I. (2008). *Learning in a new land: Immigrant students in American society*. Cambridge, MA: Harvard University Press.

Suárez-Orozco, C., Yoshikawa, H., Teranishi, R. T., and Suárez-Orozco, M. (2011). Growing up in the shadows: The developmental implications of unauthorized status. *Harvard Educational Review, 81*(3), 438–472.

Suro, R., Wilson, J. H., and Singer, A. (2011). *Immigration and poverty in America's suburbs*. Washington, DC: Brookings Institute.

Sutherland, J. A. (2011). Building an academic nation through social networks: Black immigrant men in community colleges. *Community College Journal of Research and Practice, 35*(3), 267–279.

Sy, S. R., and Romero, J. (2008). Family responsibilities among Latina college students from immigrant families. *Journal of Hispanic Higher Education, 7*(3), 212–227.

Szelenyi, K., and Chang, J. C. (2002). ERIC review: Educating immigrants: The community college role. *Community College Review, 30*(2), 55–73.

Teranishi, R. T., Suárez-Orozco, C., and Suárez-Orozco, M. (2011). Immigrants in community college: Toward greater knowledge and awareness. *Future of Children, 21*(1), 153–169.

Terenzini, P. T., Cabrera, A. F., and Bernal, E. M. (2001). *Swimming against the tide: The poor in American higher education.* College Board Research Report No. 2001-1. New York: The College Board.

Terrazas, A. (2009). *African immigrants in the United States.* Washington, DC: Migration Policy Institute.

Tierney, W. G. (1999). Models of minority college-going and retention: Cultural integrity versus cultural suicide. *Journal of Negro Education, 68*(1), 80–91.

Toossi, M. (2012). Labor force projections to 2020: A more slowly growing workforce. *Monthly Labor Review, 135*(1), 43–64.

Trueba, H. T. (1988). Culturally based explanations of minority students' academic achievement. *Anthropology and Education Quarterly, 19*(3), 270–287.

Tsai-Chae, A. H., and Nagata, D. K. (2008). Asian values and perceptions of intergenerational family conflict among Asian American students. *Cultural Diversity & Ethic Minority Psychology, 14*(3), 205–214.

Tseng, V. (2004). Family interdependence and academic adjustment in college: Youth from immigrant and U.S.-Born families. *Child Development, 75*(3), 966–983.

U.S. Bureau of Labor Statistics. (2010). *Employment projections 2008–2018, Report USDL-09-1503.* Washington, DC: U.S. Department of Labor.

U.S. Bureau of Labor Statistics. (2011). *Labor force characteristics of foreign-born workers summary, Report USDL-11-0763.* Washington, DC: U.S. Department of Labor.

U.S. Census Bureau. (2005). *Selected characteristics of the native and foreign-born populations.* Washington, DC: U.S. Census Bureau.

U.S. Census Bureau. (2009). *2009 American community survey subject tables. American fact finder.* Retrieved November 25, 2011, from factfinder.ceusus.gov.

U.S. Census Bureau. (2010). *The current population survey, 2010: Characteristics of the foreign born by generation.* Washington, DC: U.S. Census Bureau.

U.S. Census Bureau. (2012). *The current population survey, 2010: Characteristics of the foreign born by generation.* Washington, DC: U.S. Census Bureau.

U.S. Department of Education. (2004). *2003–04 national postsecondary student aid study.* Washington, DC: National Center for Education Statistics.

U.S. Department of Education. (2006). *The condition of education 2006* (NCES 2006–071). Washington, DC: National Center for Education Statistics.

U.S. Department of Education. (2008). *Community colleges: Special supplement to the condition of education 2008* (NCES 2008–033). Washington, DC: National Center for Education Statistics.

U.S. Department of Education. (2012a). *The condition of education 2012* (NCES 2012–045). Washington, DC: National Center for Education Statistics.

U.S. Department of Education. (2012b). *New Americans in postsecondary education: A profile of immigrant and second-generation American undergraduates* (NCES 2012–213). Washington, DC: National Center for Education Statistics.

Valadez, J. (1993). Cultural capital and its impact on the aspirations of nontraditional community college students. *Community College Review, 21*(3), 30–44.

Valdés, G. (2001). *Learning and not learning English: Latino students in American schools.* New York: Teachers College Press.

Vargas, J. H. (2004). *College knowledge: Addressing information barriers to college.* Boston: College Access Services: Education Resources Institute.

Venegas, K. M. (2006). Internet inequalities: Financial aid, the Internet, and low-income students. *American Behavioral Scientist, 49*(12), 1652–1669.

Vernez, G., and Abrahamse, A. (1996). *How immigrants fare in U.S. education.* Santa Monica, CA: RAND.

Waldorf, B. S., Beckhusen, J., Florax, R.J.G.M., and de Graaff, T. (2010). The role of human capital in language acquisition among immigrants in U.S. metropolitan. *Regional Science Policy and Practice, 2*(1), 39–49.

Walpole, M. (2007). Economically and educationally challenged students in higher education: Access to outcomes. *ASHE-ERIC Higher Education Report, 33*(3). San Francisco: Jossey-Bass.

Wells, R. (2008). The effect of social and cultural capital on student persistence. Are community colleges more meritocratic? *Community College Review, 36*(1), 25–46.

Wells, R. (2010). Children of immigrants and educational expectations: The roles of school composition. *Teachers College Record, 112*(6), 6–7.

Whiston, S. C., and Keller, B. K. (2004). The influences of the family of origin on career development. *The counseling psychologist, 32*(4), 493–568.

White, M. J., and Kaufman, G. (1997). Language usage, social capital, and school completion among immigrants and native-born ethnic groups. *Social Science Quarterly, 78*(2), 385–393.

Winkle-Wagner, R. (2010). *Cultural capital: The promises and pitfalls in education research.* Hoboken, NJ: Wiley Periodicals.

Wisell, T., and Champanier, L. (2010). Community colleges as critical gateways for immigrant education. *Diversity & Democracy, 13*(1), 16–17.

Yoo, H. C., and Castro, K. S. (2011). Does nativity status matter in the relationship between perceived racism and academic performance of Asian American college students? *Journal of College Student Development, 52*(2), 234–245.

Zajacova, A., Lynch, S., and Espenshade, T. (2005). Self-efficacy, stress, and academic success in college. *Research in Higher Education, 46*(6), 677–706.

Zamboanga, B. L., Raffaelli, M., and Horton, N. J. (2006). Acculturation status and heavy alcohol use among Mexican American college students: An investigation of the moderating role of gender. *Addictive Behaviors, 31*, 2188–2198.

Zarate, M. E., and Pachon, H. (2006). *Perceptions of college financial aid among California Latino youth* (Policy Brief). Los Angeles: Tomas Rivera Policy Institute.

Zeidenberg, M. (2008). Community colleges under stress. *Issues in Science and Technology, 24*(4), 53–58.

Zhou, M. (1997). Segmented assimilation: Issues, controversies, and recent research on the new second generation. *International Migration Review, 31*(4), 975–1008.

Zhou, M., and Bankston, C.L.B. III. (1994). Social capital and the adaptation of the second generation: The case of Vietnamese youth in New Orleans. *International Migration Review, 28*(4), 821–845.

Zhou, M., and Bankston, C.L.B. III. (1996). Social capital and the adaptation of the second generation: The case of Vietnamese youth in New Orleans. In A. Portes (Ed.), *The new second generation* (pp. 197–232). New York: Russell Sage Foundation.

Zhou, M., and Bankston, C.L.B. III. (1998). *Growing up American: How Vietnamese children adapt to life in the United States.* New York: Russell Sage Found.

Zhou, M., and Bankston, C.L.B. III. (2001). Family pressure and the educational experience of the daughters of Vietnamese refugees. *International Migration, 39*(4), 133–151.

Zhou, M., and Kim, S. S. (2006). Community forces, social capital, and educational achievement: The case of supplementary education in the Chinese and Korean immigrant communities. *Harvard Educational Review, 76*(1), 1–29.

Name Index

A

Abrahamse, A., 61, 93, 94
Abreu, J. M., 66
Alarcon, R., 43
Alba, R., 32, 33
Albrecht, T. J., 80, 86
Alden, L. E., 31
Allen, M. L., 67
Alsalam, N. A., 21
Alvarez, C. R., 93
American Youth Policy Forum, 55
Andrea B. Y., 68
Antonio, A. L., 35
Arnold, B., 31
Arnold, K. D., 27, 28
Auerbach, S., 56
Avery, C., 58

B

Baber, L. D., 70
Bailey, T., 64, 94, 95, 100, 106
Baker, B., 77, 79
Bankston, C., 33, 43
Bankston, C.L.B. III, 33, 41, 43, 55
Barker, M., 3
Batalova, J., 13, 14, 22, 51, 52, 83, 98, 117
Baum, S., 20, 50, 64
Beaumont, R. L., 73
Beckhusen, J., 53
Bell, A. D., 55
Beltranena, R., 53
Benesch, S., 68

Bennett, P. R., 48
Bernal, E. M., 59
Bernstein, R., 31
Berry, J. W., 30, 31, 32, 65, 70
Betts, J. R., 61
Biswas, R., 58
Bitter, C., 55
Bland, K., 118
Bleiwas, K. B., 94
Blumenthal, A., 99
Boggioni, J. A., 83
Bonstead-Bruns, M., 47
Borjas, G., 50
Bourdieu, P., 36, 37, 38, 40, 41, 45
Bourhis, R. Y., 35
Boyson, B. A., 55
Brawer, F. B., 92
Brennan, N., 118
Brettell, C. B., 68
Brilliant, J. J., 101
Bronfenbrenner, U., 27, 28, 30
Brown, F., 49
Brown, L. J., 73
Bruno, A., 83
Buddington, S., 67
Bugarin, R., 53
Butcher, K. F., 80

C

Cabrera, A. F., 55, 59
Calderone, S., 59
Callahan, R., 54, 55

Lin, N., 36, 40, 41
Lipman, F. J., 80
Liu, J. M., 41–42
Lofstrom, M., 61
Long, B. T., 58
Looney, S., 3, 4, 17, 19, 47, 58, 61, 64, 92
Lopez, J. K. 2006, 58
Lopez, M. H., 84
Lopez, M. P. 2005, 83
Lopez, N. 2003, 50, 55
Losey, K. M., 100
Louie, V. S., 50, 56, 57, 68, 72
Lumina Foundation, 79
Lutz, A., 48
Lynch, S., 64

M
MacLeod, D., 43
Magnusson, K., 74
Malagon, M., 87
Maldonado, R., 31
Malone, N. J., 80
Maramba, D. C., 62
Martin, D. C., 9
Martin, P., 3
*Martinez v. Regents of the University of
    California*, 88, 89
Massey, D. S., 43, 80
Mau, W. C., 56
McArdle, N., 94
McArthur, E., 53
McDonough, P. M., 37, 39, 59
McEwen, M. K., 68, 70
McHugh, M., 83
Melamid, E., 58, 97, 101
Menjívar, C., 53
Midgley, E., 3
Montreuil, A., 35
Morris, P. A., 27, 30
Muller, C., 54
Muñoz, S. M., 80, 87

N
Nadadur, R., 80
National Conference of State Legislatures,
    84, 85

National Immigration Law Center, 82, 85
Nava, M., 68
Nee, V., 32, 33
Neisser, U., 67
Ngo, B., 38
Nibbs, F., 68
Nienhusser, H. K., 98
Noguera, P. A., 41
Nora, A., 63
Nuñez, A. M., 34, 35, 53

O
Ogbu, J. U., 48
Oh, S. S., 25, 33, 46
Olivas, M. A., 81, 82
Oliverez, P. M., 77, 78, 80, 81, 82
Olmedo, E., 31
Ong, P. M., 41–42
Ordovensky, J. F., 2, 94
Orozco, G. L., 56
Ortiz, A. M., 69
Oseguera, L., 51
Ousey, D. L., 100
Outcalt, C. L., 39

P
Pachon, H., 59
Pannu, R., 72
Passel, J. S., 1, 2, 13, 77, 84
Passeron, J., 45
Patten, E., 14, 17, 47, 48, 50, 51, 52
Paulhus, D. L., 31
Pedersen, S., 62
Pender, M., 86
Perez Huber, L., 51, 87
Pérez, J., 93
Perez, P., 87
Perez, W., 77, 78, 80, 89
Perna, L., 55
Perna, L. W., 39, 55, 56
Perreira, K. M., 19
Perry, A. M., 82
Pew Hispanic Center, 3, 16, 17, 18, 84
Phinney, J. S., 68, 69
Piehl, A. M., 80
Pizarro, M., 69

Subject Index

A

Academic demands, immigrant students' lack of understanding concerning, 113

Academic expectations, cultural differences in, 100–101

Academic issues, coping with, 112

Acculturation, 46; defined, 65; effects on health outcomes, 67; models, 31–32; multidimensional nature of, 65–66; and self-esteem/depression, 67; theory, 30–32; unidirectional/unilinear model of, 31

Acquisition of cultural capital, 38

Act of immigration, 30

Adaptation, immigrants, 31, 46

Affordability: community colleges, 97–98; higher education, 98

Alienation/marginalization strategy, acculturation, 32

Asian American Family Conflict Scale (AAFCS), 66

Asian Indian immigrants, college major preferences, 72–73

Asian Values Scale (AVS), 66

Asians: college student identities and ethnic identities, 69; development of racial and ethnic identity in, 69; and foreign-born U.S. population, 13, 14; parental influence on academic achievement of, 56; racial and ethnic identity development, 68

Assimilation, 46; defined, 32; reception in, 34; selective acculturation, 32–33; theory, 32–34; and upward social mobility, 32; into the urban underclass, 32

Assimilation/Americanized strategy, acculturation, 31–32

Asylees, 9

B

Baccalaureate and Beyond Longitudinal Study (B&B), 110–111

Barriers to parental involvement in college decisions, 56–57

Beginning Postsecondary Students Longitudinal Study (BPS), 110–111

Bidirectional model of acculturation, 31

Black sub-Saharan African immigrant adult students, career development, 73

Blacks: college student identities and ethnic identities, 69; development of racial and ethnic identity in, 69; and foreign-born U.S. population, 14; heritage cultural orientation, 67

Bourdieu's social and cultural capital, 36–39

"Bridge to Allied Health Careers" courses, at CIET, 103

C

Campus environment, and immigrant student difficulties, 114

Career aspirations and development, 72–73; and collegiate experience of immigrant students, 72–73

preparation, 54; ESL programs/ placement, 54–55; and immediate surroundings, 53–54; language proficiency, acquiring, 54–55

English-language proficiency, *See also* Limited English proficiency (LEP): and access to higher education, 52–55

Equal Protection Clause, U.S. Constitution, 89

ESL instruction, 101

ESOL (English for Speakers of Other Languages) classes, CIET, 102

Ethnic identity, 69

Ethnic peer networks, 112; membership, 44; and social ties, 113

Europe, and foreign-born U.S. population, 13

Exosystem, social-ecological model, 28–29

F

Faculty and peer interactions, cultural differences in, 101

Family Literacy program, CIET, 102–103

Family responsibilities, and college retention of Latinas, 63

Federation for American Immigration Reform (FAIR), 88–89

Financial aid, 57–60, 113; information found on the Internet, 59–60; lack of knowledge of resources, 58–59; navigating the system, 58

Financial management guidance, 101

First-generation immigrants, 9

Foreign-born, use of term, 7–8, 12

Foreign-born workers: college-educated labor force, 22; earning rates, 22; educational attainment gap, 21; and growth in U.S. population, 21; high-school education, 21

Free Application for Federal Student Aid (FAFSA), 58–59

Frequency of returning home, and acculturation, 67

Future research suggestions, 110–112

G

Generational status, and access to higher education, 48–49

"Green card" holders, 8

H

Habitus, defined, 37

Health issues, guidance sought about, 101

Health risk behaviors, and college students, 66–67

High-school education, foreign-born workers, 21

High School Longitudinal Study (HSL), 110–111

Higher education: affordability, 98; and English language proficiency, 52–55; financial aid, 57–60; generational status, 48–49; immigrant student access to, 47–60; parental involvement and expectations, 55–57; as pathway for immigrant integration into American society, 1; socioeconomic status, 49–51; and undocumented immigrant students, 77–90

Higher education access, and English language proficiency, 52–55

Higher Education Act of 1965, 80

Hispanics: and foreign-born U.S. population, 14; heritage-cultural practices, 67

Housing guidance, 101

Humanitarian migrants, 9

I

Illegal immigrants, 8

Illegal Immigration Reform and Immigrant Responsibility Act (IIRIRA), 81, 82, 89

Immigrant assimilation: context of reception in, 34; student persistence, applicability of segmented theory in, 34–35

Immigrant-origin students: acculturation, 67; and cultural capital, 39; persistence of, 65; and transformation of educational/labor landscapes, 45

Suburban areas, and immigrants, 13
Suinn-Lew Asian Self-Identity
    Acculturation Scale (SL-ASIA), 66

T

Temporary residents, 8–9
Third-generation immigrants, 10
Transgenerational impact period,
    immigration, 30
Tuition policy, community colleges, 97–98

U

Unauthorized immigrants, 8
Undocumented immigrant students, 8,
    77–90; background on, 79–80; federal
    legislation, 80–84; and in-state tuition/
    attendance at public postsecondary
    institutions, 98; opposition to in-state
    tuition rates for, 88–89; state approaches
    to, 84–88
Undocumented immigrants, 6, 8
Unidirectional/unilinear model of
    acculturation, 31

United States, as country of immigrants, 1
Upward mobility, 1, 32–33, 48
U.S. Census American Community Survey
    and Current Population Survey, 110–111
U.S. Census Bureau, 12; American
    Community Survey (2010), 13

V

Vietnam, and foreign-born U.S.
    population, 13
Vietnamese students, acculturation, 33–34

W

Westchester Community College (Valhalla
    NY), 103
Whites: college student identities and
    ethnic identities, 69; development of
    racial and ethnic identity in, 68–69;
    Hispanic, 3, 20; non-Hispanic, 3, 14,
    22; parental influence on academic
    achievement of, 56; racial and ethnic
    identity development, 68
Workers, foreign-born, 21–22

About the Authors

Eunyoung Kim is an assistant professor of the Higher Education Program in the Department of Education Leadership, Management, and Policy at Seton Hall University. Kim has several publications and numerous presentations, including a recent article about the role of campus peer networks in ethnic minority immigrant students' persistence in college. Her research areas include the transition from secondary to postsecondary education, minority students' college access and success, immigrant student racial/ethnic identity development, diversity and equity in higher education, and international students' adjustment. Over the past several years, Kim's scholarship has focused on identifying and describing the needs of underserved student populations in an effort to promote their psychosocial growth, enhance their social and economic mobility, and eradicate their invisibility and marginalization. In another line of inquiry, her work examines the impacts of cultural and social capital on student learning outcomes and college persistence. She currently serves as director of the MA program in College Student Personnel Administration at Seton Hall University and teaches a wide array of graduate courses including College Student Affairs Administration, American College Student, and Diversity in Higher Education. Kim was the recipient of the 2007–2008 Paul P. Fidler Grant sponsored by the National Resource Center for the First Experience and Students in Transition and a fellow of the 2007–2008 ASHE/Lumina Foundation Dissertation Fellowship. She has also been selected as a 2013 Emerging Scholar by the American College Personnel Association

(ACPA). Kim received a bachelor's degree in political science from Ewha Womans University in the Republic of Korea and both an MA in teaching English as an international language and a PhD in educational organization and leadership from the University of Illinois at Urbana-Champaign.

Jeannette Díaz is a PhD candidate in the Higher Education Program of the Department of Education Leadership, Management, and Policy at Seton Hall University. She has worked as a legal counsel and consultant on immigration issues for a number of years. Ms. Díaz is an attorney admitted to the New York State Bar in 1986, the U.S. District Court, Southern District of New York in 1995, and the Supreme Court of the United States in 1996. She received her EdS in bilingual/bicultural education at Seton Hall University in 2002, her JD from Brooklyn Law School in 1985, and her BA from New York University in 1982. Throughout her twenty-five-year legal career, Ms. Díaz has worked with the immigrant communities (documented and undocumented) as a student intern at Catholic Charities, in private practice, and as Program Director/Supervising attorney at the Citizens Advice Bureau in the Bronx. Her research interests lie in policies and practices associated with access to, persistence, and completion of postsecondary education for undocumented immigrants and the impact of immigration policies on their educational attainment and employment.

About the ASHE Higher Education Report Series

Since 1983, the ASHE (formerly ASHE-ERIC) Higher Education Report Series has been providing researchers, scholars, and practitioners with timely and substantive information on the critical issues facing higher education. Each monograph presents a definitive analysis of a higher education problem or issue, based on a thorough synthesis of significant literature and institutional experiences. Topics range from planning to diversity and multiculturalism, to performance indicators, to curricular innovations. The mission of the Series is to link the best of higher education research and practice to inform decision making and policy. The reports connect conventional wisdom with research and are designed to help busy individuals keep up with the higher education literature. Authors are scholars and practitioners in the academic community. Each report includes an executive summary, review of the pertinent literature, descriptions of effective educational practices, and a summary of key issues to keep in mind to improve educational policies and practice.

The Series is one of the most peer reviewed in higher education. A National Advisory Board made up of ASHE members reviews proposals. A National Review Board of ASHE scholars and practitioners reviews completed manuscripts. Six monographs are published each year and they are approximately 144 pages in length. The reports are widely disseminated through Jossey-Bass and John Wiley & Sons, and they are available online to subscribing institutions through Wiley Online Library (http://wileyonlinelibrary.com).

Call for Proposals

The ASHE Higher Education Report Series is actively looking for proposals. We encourage you to contact one of the editors, Dr. Kelly Ward (kaward@wsu.edu) or Dr. Lisa Wolf-Wendel (lwolf@ku.edu), with your ideas.

Recent Titles

ORDER FORM SUBSCRIPTION AND SINGLE ISSUES

DISCOUNTED BACK ISSUES:

Use this form to receive 20% off all back issues of *ASHE Higher Education Report*.
All single issues priced at **$23.20** (normally $29.00)

TITLE	ISSUE NO.	ISBN

Call 888-378-2537 or see mailing instructions below. When calling, mention the promotional code JBNND to receive your discount. For a complete list of issues, please visit www.josseybass.com/go/aehe

SUBSCRIPTIONS: (1 YEAR, 6 ISSUES)

☐ New Order   ☐ Renewal

U.S.	☐ Individual: $174	☐ Institutional: $307
CANADA/MEXICO	☐ Individual: $174	☐ Institutional: $367
ALL OTHERS	☐ Individual: $210	☐ Institutional: $418

Call 888-378-2537 or see mailing and pricing instructions below.
Online subscriptions are available at www.onlinelibrary.wiley.com

ORDER TOTALS:

Issue / Subscription Amount: $ _____

Shipping Amount: $ _____
(for single issues only – subscription prices include shipping)

Total Amount: $ _____

SHIPPING CHARGES:
First Item $6.00
Each Add'l Item $2.00

(No sales tax for U.S. subscriptions. Canadian residents, add GST for subscription orders. Individual rate subscriptions must be paid by personal check or credit card. Individual rate subscriptions may not be resold as library copies.)

BILLING & SHIPPING INFORMATION:

☐ **PAYMENT ENCLOSED:** *(U.S. check or money order only. All payments must be in U.S. dollars.)*

☐ **CREDIT CARD:**   ☐ VISA   ☐ MC   ☐ AMEX

Card number _____ Exp. Date_____

Card Holder Name_____ Card Issue # _____

Signature _____ Day Phone_____

☐ **BILL ME:** *(U.S. institutional orders only. Purchase order required.)*

Purchase order # _____
Federal Tax ID 13559302 • GST 89102-8052

Name_____

Address_____

Phone_____ E-mail_____

Copy or detach page and send to: **John Wiley & Sons, One Montgomery Street, Suite 1200, San Francisco, CA 94104-4594**

Order Form can also be faxed to: **888-481-2665**

PROMO JBNND